THE SECRETS TO YOUR
WIN

THE SECRETS TO YOUR
WIN

...simple little things that make all the difference

TEMITOPE IBRAHIM

Published by Willow Books, Newark, DE 19702.
Direct all inquiries to publicatons@willowbooks.com

The author has tried to recreate events and conversations from her recollection of them. In order to protect the privacy of those mentioned in the book, names and identifying details have been changed.

Editors: Douglas Imaralu & Shade Sabitu
Author's Photograph: Karen McDaniel
Front Cover & Packaging: Willow Books
Cover Art: ThaiPrayBoy

Paperback ISBN: 978-0-9990497-0-9

Available in E-book also

DEDICATION

To the winner in you: rise up!

ACKNOWLEDGEMENTS

To The One who makes impossibilities possible: to You I owe everything. If only I could title the book as authored by GOD. I only shared what You revealed to me. Thank you for every word you speak and every thought you inspire.

To my dear husband: thank you for believing in me way before I could see anything. I couldn't have asked for a better crown; you beautify me always.

To my boys: you sacrificed alongside me on this one. Thanks for the many night checkups and kisses. I love you guys.

To my parents: you were a solid and healthy foundation. I appreciate every experience, they all shaped me well.

To my wonderful editors at Willow Books: what more can I say, you made this better than a book.

To all those who poured into me at one time or the other, to those who are still pouring and to all those who helped draw out of me what was hidden in me. I am eternally grateful!

And to you who is reading this book: Thanks for picking up the book, you will definitely be better for it. Now, let your WIN begin.

"Life is simple with GOD"

CONTENTS

1

GOD DESIRES

GOD desires that you win! As a matter of fact, you couldn't desire your win more than He desires it for you. Like a parent desires great success for their children, even much so, GOD desires that you are victorious in all you do. His desire is that you win in every situation, over every challenge, and through every circumstance of your life. He wants you to win in everything. The type of win He desires for you is not temporary nor sporadic; it's a growing win. The kind that can be qualified as 'leaping from glory to glory'; a win that is constant, unwavering and unbeatable. His desire is a win that transcends all things and all realms. He doesn't want you triumphing in some areas and failing in others. Truthfully, no parent desires that for their children, how much more GOD?

My husband and I have two boys and they make up the center of our world, right in line after Jesus and each other. They couldn't possibly desire to be greater than we desire greatness for them. I say that, not as a parent who will not be satisfied with whatever her children become in life, but as a parent who knows the potential GOD has put in every man, and understands no matter how high they stake their claim, the possibility for even higher remains within their reach... if they'll just dare to dream. Having said that, it does not mean we impose on our children, nor does it mean we will dictate the path they'll take in life. It simply means, we want the best for them and will love them through their choices; good, bad, and ugly. But we pray hard that the bad and ugly will be few and in between. In the same way, GOD will not impose His desires for our win upon us. He roots for us, hopes on us and is always directing us so the bad and ugly are few and in between, if at all necessary. He knows we can win, and we will, if we would only trust Him. He, however, prefers that we are willing and consenting participants to this desire. Have you ever tried forcing a child to do something? There's a lot of whining and crying involved; it's not pleasant for all parties involved. But when a child is willing, it can be a real joy to experience.

GOD desires a complete win. Some folks argue that salvation and heaven are the win. They believe GOD is only interested in saving us so we can make our way back home to heaven. But every time I hear such thoughts, I find myself asking this question "Why would GOD send us into earth just so we can find our way back into heaven?" It would seem futile to leave home for no other purpose than just returning home. There is a purpose to being on earth! I will propose to you our being saved jumpstarts the fullness of His joy over us and making it to heaven certainly would crown that joy. But I truly believe, GOD's joy can only be full, in its entirety over our lives, when we win here on earth as well as in heaven. It's important for us to understand GOD is not only interested in our win, as it pertains to salvation and heaven, but a win that includes victories as you journey this earth. With GOD, it doesn't matter where you are; a winner is a winner. If you are only looking forward to heaven as your win, you are short changing yourself because you can start winning right here, right now. Why defer your win?

> If you are only looking forward to heaven as your win, you are short changing yourself.

I have come to understand that those who only look forward to heaven as their win do so because they don't yet know how to win here on earth. And so, as consolation, they defer their victory to when they gain entrance through the pearly gates. The truth is, if they knew how to win now, they would. Learn how to win now and you wouldn't have to (or want to or need to) defer your winning experience until you get to heaven. Jesus didn't only win through death, He won living as well. When we focus solely on heaven as our win, we are basically embracing only half the treasures secured for us in the sacrifice of Jesus Christ. His life was just as significant as His death in securing our victory. His life was a prototype for ours; He showed us how the manufacturer's model called Man ought to operate and exist in this realm.

WHAT IT MEANS TO WIN

It's important to get a clear understanding of what it means to win here on earth; not according to the world and societal definitions, but according to GOD and His ultimate purpose. Winning with GOD simply means living a victorious life. And a victorious life can be expressed as living a life that tallies with GOD's intention for you. GOD has a plan for your life, and He brought you forth solely for that purpose. You can't win without fulfilling that purpose. To attempt to win, outside of purpose, would be like scrubbing the bathroom with a fork _— it just won't work. The fork, the bathroom, the person doing the scrubbing and even innocent bystanders listening to the shrieking noise that will be produced — all lose in this futile effort. The glory of the fork can only be displayed when it is being used on the table, for the purpose for which it was created. When in its proper place and in proper use, the fork wins, the plate wins, the table wins, the person using the fork appropriately wins, and the bathroom that has now been saved from the screeching scratches also wins. To win connotes that one is excelling in the purpose to which they are called. Your win is dependent on the purpose for your life. To exist outside of that purpose is to be as frustrated as the fork would be scrubbing the bathroom. But there is a *greater purpose* behind every purpose. You'll soon see what I mean.

•••••••

I sat at a conference once, looking at the huge stage and listening to the different speakers that were presenting. I dreamt of a day that I, too, would stand on such a stage to share what GOD would place in my heart for that time. I looked on, with awe in my eyes and faith roused up in me, when suddenly, I heard a small whisper ask me, "why do you want to speak on this stage?" I was perplexed at the question. I thought to myself, "isn't it a good thing I desire such a stage, if I have a message?" I thought my desire was in line with my purpose, so having such a desire seemed appropriate. But I had learnt, when GOD asks questions, usually it's because your thoughts do not align with His. And so, I began to search my motives and I found all my reasons for wanting to be up there somehow didn't fly. My motives were riddled with fame, making a name for myself, and wanting the accolades that comes with being considered an elite speaker. As I found each answer within me, I slumped with guilt. After a bit of a pause, I responded to God with words I now know could only have been GOD speaking through me: 'whatever my current reasons are for desiring such a stage, I only want to be up there for the right reasons'. And immediately I heard Him say, "the only good reason to be up there is to glorify me".

It was then I realized that there is a *Purpose* for my purpose; there is an ultimate Purpose behind every purpose of man. Our individual purposes are a means to an ultimate end. Greater than the individual purpose of each person; our ultimate, "forever-Purpose" is to display and prove GOD. Yes! Your most profound 'why' is to manifest GOD! The only good reason to do anything at all is to show, for all to see, the wonders of The One who created you, and to prove His majesty in and through everything you do. When we do that, GOD is glorified. GOD is proven through our lives and His will is established in the earth as it is in heaven. GOD's plan is that you win and it gives Him great satisfaction when you do, because to win is to prove GOD!

OUT TO GET YOU

Some people think life was designed particularly against them. They think nothing good comes to them and that GOD has purposefully rigged the system just so they would fail! They think GOD sits where He is and plots against them, just to frustrate their existence. But how can that be? Have you ever seen a loving father seeking to frustrate his child? You won't find one, ever. The qualifiers here are love, father & child. Love is how a father deals with his child and love is how GOD deals with you. His love runs deep for all His children. It's the kind of love that drove Him to the cross to permanently secure your win. Why die for someone whom you want to fail? Do you think His dying for you was a cover up for His real intentions? If His purpose was your failure, there will be no need to conceal it. Even if He came right out and said He wanted us to fail, who could question Him? Who could ask Him what and why He does what He does? His death on the cross is enough proof He wants you to win. His love for you goes beyond words and His desire for your win goes beyond comprehension. So deep is His love, our minds could never fully comprehend it. So sure is His desire, He went to all lengths to make it irrevocable. He died so you can win against all odds. Enough thinking GOD has rigged it all against you. The truth is: when we misuse a thing, we are bound to think it's difficult or hard or simply not meant for us.

When my son was much younger, he tried opening a bottle of juice and was very frustrated when the cap wouldn't turn. He knew there was good stuff in there and wanted its content, but every attempt to open the bottle failed. He was twisting the cap clockwise! That's the opposite direction when you want to open a bottle, but he didn't know at the time. So, he threw a fit. He was so frustrated, he didn't even entertain the thought of twisting the cap the other way. That's how we are many times, throwing a fit at life, ignorant of the fact we're merely "twisting" it wrongly. We know there are many good things in life to experience, express and manifest, but because we're twisting it wrongly, we're not getting the desired results. Many people live life in the opposite direction of the manufacturer's intention and expect it to still work appropriately. It won't! Things will not change simply because you are throwing a fit, while stubbornly heading towards the wrong direction.

•••••••

"GOD is out to get me" a man once said to me. Unfortunately, I know he's not the only one that thinks this way. It is easy to think GOD is set against us when we are doing everything wrong and expecting everything to be right. Especially when you see other people living their own dreams, soaring in their own light and 'drinking the content of their own bottles'. When it seems things aren't working out for you, you may begin to wonder why life is teasing you. Or worse yet, you may feel like life is a punishment and GOD is the one doing the punishing. I'm pretty sure my son had these similar thoughts, seeing time and time again how others were opening similar bottles and getting to the goodies within their bottles. He had seen them access the content of the bottle, through the cap, but somehow it wasn't working for him. He had been inspired by other people's achievements, but in that moment, life must have seemed hard because he tried to no avail. No matter what he must have concluded was the root of the problem, it didn't change the fact he just didn't know how to open the bottle. The truth will not change regardless of how we feel or what we think it looks like. We must learn to work life as designed by GOD. The problem with thinking GOD is out to get you is you will always feel defeated, even before starting.

God desires that you know the truth and begin to triumph over the lies that have plagued you. His desire is for you to work life armed with these truths so you will not jeopardize yourself in an already secured victory. Regardless of how you feel about it, life hasn't been rigged against you; it isn't a tease; and it isn't a punishment. In fact, it's an assignment. And like every mission that must be successfully accomplished, there is a well thought-out and mapped-out plan to help guide the journey. If only you'll follow it, you'll find life was designed for you and not against you. The truth you know is the truth that will set you free.

THE PLOT TWIST

Life is simple. That's how GOD designed it and He wants you to know this. Right about now, I bet you're thinking, 'what world does she live in?' But hear me well; I said life is simple, not easy. Just like the cap on the bottle my son was trying to open, life is simple when worked right. If you can find the way it was designed to work, you would have found everything and will be triumphant over all things. Let me clarify a little bit further: life is simple with GOD. Life was designed to work in GOD. He is the difference maker; His involvement in your life makes all the difference. And little wonder why; He created you and the life you are living. He is the manufacturer and knows how both ought to work for optimal glory. If you can live life as designed by The Creator, you will experience life leaping from glory to glory and victory to victory. As long as man can live life following the guiding principles set forth by GOD, it is simple. Living life outside of these guiding principles, however, is where men find life too complicated to deal with.

Life is simple, not easy.

I remember the days that simple multiplication used to confuse me. The concept of 5x5 was the most difficult thing to me in 1st grade. I just couldn't wrap my mind around it and I can't tell you how many times I wished upon a star that mathematics would no longer be a subject; as well as reading, comprehension, spelling… all school subjects, basically (well, maybe except for arts and P.E.). I just didn't want a part of any of it. Those wishes obviously fell to the ground since none of those subjects went away. But no matter how complicated I thought those subjects were, they were only complicated because I didn't get it. Once I got the concept behind them though, they became the simplest things ever. Life will continue to seem complicated until you get it. Unfortunately, many people do not strive to master life the way they ought to. Life is about discovering and unleashing the giant within. We create who we are, even the very person we were created to be, only when we discover what is on the inside — the efficient power of the Holy Spirit that works in us. When we come face to face with this power, embrace it and allow it to have its perfect work in us, we will begin to live life as designed and you'll be amazed at its simplicity.

Why then does life seem complicated?

Life seems complicated because an enemy is in the mix. We have a tireless adversary who is angry about his permanent loss. He works so hard to skew our perception of his irrevocable loss and our irrevocable victory. He wants nothing more than to take your win and give you his defeat. But it is a done deal; it will never happen!

I used to wander why the enemy tried so hard, despite his known fate. Why does he go all out for a battle he has already lost? This kept me perplexed until I heard Pricilla Shirer tell the following story about her son:

> Her son, Jerry Shirer, was a baseball player. On this particular occasion, he was feeling defeated because he heard who the opposing team was and how good they were. Those boys were intimidating. According to Pricilla, they seemed bred for the game. You know, the kind raised on the baseball field, with first words that were probably 'mittens'. So, on this day, Jerry, with his head down, walked by the opponent's dugout and overheard them say, with much awe in their voices, "that's Jerry Shirer, remember him?". They went on describing one of Jerry's incredible plays against another team. The best part: he could hear the amazement mixed with fear in their voices.
>
> Pricilla said Jerry suddenly found strength in his neck to hold his head up high. She told the story to emphasize the difference between what we think the enemy is saying about us and what they are actually saying about us. If we only heard what the enemy really thought of us, our heads would be held up two whole feet above our bodies; higher than high. But as she took us through the story, I couldn't help

but wonder why the opposing team still showed up. They were obviously in dread of Jerry, yet they showed up! And in that moment, it occurred to me that even the enemy operates on hope. Though they were defeated in their hearts, and afraid of the ball pitching giant, they hoped maybe, just maybe, he would be off his game that day. And on that sliver of hope, they showed up.

Winning some is all the devil is after; just winning some days. He's not counting on a total win, though he fights like he does. He knows his loss is irrevocable. He knows the win is already signed, sealed, and delivered to us by the precious blood of Christ. But like Jerry's opponent, he is hoping his presence will scare you enough to cause you to give up your win.

You must understand why he is so sore against you. You see, the devil was an angel of light, turned rogue due to pride. Imagine the degradation... he who was once light, turned to darkness. Darkness has nothing to offer but to hide sores, cloak wickedness and conceal unsightly things. Who wouldn't be constantly enraged when weighed down by such? And for a being who once tasted light's airy, weightless, creative and life-giving gift, you can be sure of his frustration. It is better to not have tasted bliss at all than to taste and lose it; all by one's own doing. He once enjoyed life in abundance and now is condemned to utter darkness by his own choosing. Why wouldn't he be jealous of you – you are the creation that owns the heart of the Master. He gets none of it and you get all of GOD's heart; His whole heart is always turned towards you.

What is man that You are mindful of him, and the son of man that You visit him? For You have made him a little lower than the angels, [yet] You have crowned him with glory and honor. You have made him to have dominion over the works of Your hands; You have put all things under his feet, All sheep and oxen— Even the beasts of the field, The birds of the air, And the fish of the sea That pass through the paths of the seas. O Lord, our Lord, how excellent is Your name in all the earth! (Psalm 8:4-9 NKJV)

It is also interesting to think that man, who was created lower than angels, would by choice — a desire rather than an innate compulsion — love GOD better and more intimately than an angel, who by the same choice fell from grace. It helps to see this in the context of feuding enemies. This reminds me of a satirical representation of an infringement settlement between tech giants Samsung and Apple. In the illustration, Samsung paid a settlement of about $1.5 million to Apple, in pennies! Whether it was true or not, doesn't really matter, but it does help to understand the *suck-it-to-you-ness* that can be activated in feuds. So, I'd like to speculate that GOD's move to create man was a *suck-it-to-you* move to ridicule the devil and his selfish desires. There you have it! The eternal slap in the face of the devil and the reason behind the burning enmity: it is personal.

So, you see this vendetta is no joke. He takes it very seriously. A divine slap is infinitely painful, and so he can't, and will never, get over it. He has vowed to steal us away from our first love by painting us a different picture than what is true, all so we too can turn our backs on GOD. But I pray we never take that bait. I always say the enemy is not innovative; he can't create. Only the Spirit of GOD creates and innovates. So, his tricks are the same old tricks, from way back in the garden of Eden: throwing false choices at you to entice you. It's like fishing; if only the fish would stop taking the bait.

THE REAL SETUP

Although the enemy works tirelessly to paint us a different picture, here is the real set up:

> *"As the rain and the snow come down from heaven, and do not return to it without watering the earth and making it bud and flourish, so that it yields seed for the sower and bread for the eater, so is my word that goes out from my mouth: It will not return to me empty, but will accomplish what I desire and achieve the purpose for which I sent it."* *(Isaiah 55:10-11 NIV)*

According to the scripture above, GOD's words, no matter how outrageous or insignificant, will be fulfilled. His words never go unfulfilled. Not ever! When GOD said *"Light"* in the beginning, according to the book of Genesis, there was no other option but for that word to be actualized into the brightness we call light today. He created all things by His spoken word. Everything you see, and even the things whose existence you can't imagine, were created by His word. That includes you! Now, this the real setup: You are a living breathing word of GOD! And since His word can never go unfulfilled, you can never go unfulfilled. You cannot but win! And, as the Word says, you will not return to Him empty!

Come what may, you are not empty. Though the mountains roar and the valleys threaten to swallow you up, know this with a mule-like confidence and an unrelenting assurance: You are not empty. No matter what happens, you will accomplish His desire for you and achieve the purpose for which He spoke you into existence. The real setup is you are made! If you were not created by word, there may have been a chance at failure. But the core of your being is the word of GOD; it is the very material you were formed out of. And you heard Him say "you will not return to Him without accomplishing the purpose for which you were created". You cannot but win; you are word! And remember *"No word from GOD shall be without power or impossible of fulfillment"*

You are living breathing word of GOD.

But then there is a part for you to play. I'll explain with this illustration. A farmer who expects a bountiful harvest must first sow and then await the rain. He sure doesn't have control over the rain but he must sow to expect a harvest. Expecting a harvest without sowing would be day-dreaming. Sowing is his responsibility in the process. And even after he has sown, and the harvest starts to come in, he must guard his land against weeds, pests and thieves, otherwise his harvest will be impacted. If wild beasts are allowed to graze on the land, and thieves are consciously or unconsciously welcomed, surely his harvest will be plundered. He must guard what he's been given!

Even so, your life was given to you. You must not only use what is given to you, you must guard and protect it in order to win. It is required of us, as stewards of our lives, to be faithful to the Word that called us into being, ensuring to prove it accurate and true with everything we do. We must guard the land of our lives from weeds and beasts and thieves and crows so our harvest may be full, and above all, our win complete and entire. GOD desires that you know this.

2

DO YOU BELIEVE?

One major part in bringing GOD's desire to fulfillment in your life is belief. You must believe His desire for you and align your desire with His to see them play out in your life. You simply cannot experience what you have not first believed. Even when it happens right under your nose, you will miss it, if you refuse to first believe. No matter how amazing a person's victory is, the first thing that had to happen was them believing in that very thing. You cannot attain what you cannot imagine possible.

As Nicodemus was famous for not understanding what it meant to be born again, I ought to make the records for my ignorance on (and stubbornness against) the subject of speaking in tongues. I just couldn't wrap my mind around it in the beginning. I used to wonder why GOD needed a language of His own, when He gave us all these different languages already. It now seems like a no brainer, but believe me when I say it was a stronghold for a long time. And for as long as I didn't believe, it wasn't going to happen for me. The reason is this: GOD will not give pearls to pigs. And I am by no means agreeing to being a pig but I can tell you truthfully that I would have acted like one if He gave me a precious gift before I believed in it or desired it.

Today, by the unfailing grace of GOD, I have the gift of speaking in tongues; but I'll save the story of how all that came about for another day. The first thing GOD had to do however, to bring to this reality, was to get me to believe in what I thought was impossible. To me, it was impossible to speak in tongues, but with GOD it was a certainty. Remember He won't impose; so, He spent time reasoning it out with me until I got it. And when I finally believed in its possibility, I couldn't wait… I wanted the gift immediately. I yearned for it, prayed earnestly about it, and finally one day it came spilling out. I remember that day vividly because I couldn't shut up. Even when my mouth was closed, it was going on inside me. I seemed like I had another mouth and I couldn't control it. Everywhere I went that day, it was going on; at work, at school, at home, during conversations, when I was working on tasks…everywhere and in everything, it was going on. My mouth had been unbuttoned and I was super glad.

•••••••

Do you believe GOD? I mean, like really believe GOD? Do you truly have faith in what you say you believe? Or do you simply think you know and profess, without true faith in what you are saying? I have found that there were days I didn't quite believe, though I thought I did. And this is where it gets tricky — when you think you believe but you really don't. It's hard to accept that we fool ourselves, but we do it all the time. I mean, how can one know the word, profess the word, even pray the word, and still not believe? Doesn't that qualify as fooling one's self? Thank GOD there's hope! Thank GOD there's always a solution with Jesus.

CAN GOD

A man once came to Jesus seeking healing for his demon-possessed son. It's important to note Jesus didn't seek this man out. The man sought Jesus. And when he met face to face with Jesus, he asked, "*If you can do anything, take pity on us and help us*". "If you *can*," he said. I'll paraphrase Jesus' response: "If I can? Are you asking about my capability to do? My ability to do is not in question here, your faith is" I then began to wonder, 'Was this man not convinced Jesus could heal before he packed up his son and brought him before the Lord?" Surely, the man had heard of Jesus and was convinced He could perform miracles. Or why else would he spend his time coming to Christ, if he thought Jesus couldn't? If we're honest with ourselves, we've all asked this very question at one time or another. Let's settle it here.

Sometimes we have hiccups believing GOD at His word. This

might happen because we've tried other avenues, or even tried other beliefs, and things didn't quite work out the way we expect. Take, for example, the man with the demon-possessed son. He had tried the disciples first. He believed enough in the power of healing and brought his son to the disciples. But they couldn't cast out the demon. This must have put a bit of a dent in his faith. After that failed attempt, he was probably feeling skeptical about trying Jesus. The blow to his faith is evident in his words to Jesus. He says to Him "If you *can* do anything, take pity on us and help us" He was probably starting to question both the authenticity of the disciples and Jesus at that point.

I see many of us in this man. This happens to us too many a times. When we believe and things somehow don't work the way we hope, we peg it against GOD and it dampens the potency of our faith. We judge GOD by people. We say things like, 'if they truly are His people, they should be able to do something about my situation'. And when these 'people of God' are unable to perform our desires, we take it out on GOD.

The same thing must have happened at the mount where Elijah gathered all the prophets of Baal and all the prophets of Asherah for a show down. The records of this occurrence begin to give us a sense of what the prophets of Baal were feeling and doing. We also get a sense of what Elijah was doing. But have you given some thought to what the people were doing? What must have been going through the minds of the people who stood on the side lines, watching the spectacle? Let me help you paint a picture: imagine all the people standing in excitement, waiting on the show down to begin, and hoping to prove what they think they know to be the truth — Baal is god (at this point, they had deserted the Lord and the majority were Baal worshippers). Suddenly, someone shouts from the back of the crowd "Today we will know that Baal is god", then the crowd cheers in excitement. Just as suddenly as the first shout was heard, another voice confidently proclaims; "Let the true god be proven today". The crowd erupts in cheers. Majority cheered because they were on 'Team Baal'; some joined in for fear of not being in the majority. There was also a handful of people whose heart began to whisper and wonder what the outcome of this 'battle' would be. Then the prophets of Baal begin their rituals. They cry and shout, slit their hands and lance their bodies, as is the custom. In excitement, and support for the prophets of Baal, the crowd also join in the ceremonial exercises, cutting themselves and chanting for Baal to respond. They scream louder, as Elijah encourages them to try harder to arouse their god. 'Just in case he hasn't heard your cries yet', mocks Elijah. "Maybe he had a long line of people he was attending to and didn't understand the urgency of what was needed," Elijah says. But soon the excitement turns to quiet, and disappointment sets on the faces of all those on team Baal, as there was no response; Baal doesn't respond. The shouting and begging goes on from morning till evening, according to the record, and nothing, absolutely nothing happens. At the end of the day, the crowd is weary, exhausted, and disappointed.

By the time Elijah finally calls their attention his way, they were already drained of hope. Their expectation shattered, with nothing else to hold on to. They had done all they could, to the one they knew as god, yet nothing happened. The exhaustion, mixed with frustration on their faces, would not allow them to even hope for a miracle. At this point, they were asking, just like that man asked Jesus: "can Jehovah send fire?"

Past failed experiences can unravel one's faith and lead to one questioning the possibility of even simple things happening. Some people even doubt their own journey, just by witnessing other people's defeat. Imagine being in Elijah's shoes and doubting GOD, just because Baal failed. We must be careful not to judge GOD based on anything or anyone else. You cannot judge The Judge! Sometimes we find ourselves in the dark and losing sight of the hope in GOD. And others who are in the dark begin to whisper doubt to you. It doesn't matter who's in the dark with you, or who went through the dark before you, or how convincing they told of their personal horrors, "you must never doubt in the dark what GOD told you in the light".

Thankfully, Elijah didn't get discouraged by the countenance of the crowd. Instead, he went to work. He picked up twelve stones, repaired the altar, dug trenches around the altar, placed the sacrifice on the wood and watered it well enough to saturate the hearts of the people with hope again. And when he called on GOD, fire fell and licked up everything on and near the alter, even the earth. One minute, they saw everything right in front of them, and then the next minute, they saw nothing but a crater in the earth, as proof of the fire. Imagine the awakened amazement! Their countenance went from "not interested" to "did that just happen", in the twinkling of an eye. Many an eye were rubbed, as people took second glances at crater hoping to see it was all a joke. But it was real; Jehovah had answered by fire. Some fell on their knees, and even some on their faces, bowing down in awe of what they just witnessed. Elijah didn't have to convince them any longer; they were sure of it. The fire had licked up all the doubt in their heart, along with everything else.

John records *"Blessed are they that have not seen and yet have believed"*. My interpretation: blessed are those who believe even though their current view is contrary to what they dare to believe. They are specially blessed because they have not allowed reality to rob them of what their eyes see in faith.

WILL GOD

Most people are convinced about GOD's ability to do. They do not doubt His might, the span of His authority or His majesty over all. I believe that too! However, where I used to get stuck was whether He would. Many have settled the issue of the "can-ness" of GOD but most have not settled the issue of His willingness. We know GOD can bless, move mountains, split the seas, raise the dead, change lives; the list goes on. But the main question that plagues most people is this: "Will GOD do it for me"?

That question used to stop me in my tracks whenever I prayed to heaven. For many years, the question would cause me to swallow my prayers, halfway through, because, by my own assessments, I did not meet the requirements of those that could receive from GOD. I felt 'my credentials' reduced the chances of getting whatever I wanted to ask. The question of the willingness of GOD to do is one many have not answered. Let's do that now.

Imagine if a loving father says to his son: "let me take you to the ice cream shop." And on getting there, the boy, amazed by the infinite possibilities, engages himself in the difficult task of deciding what he wants. He then goes to his dad and says, "I want cookie dough mixed with mint flavored ice cream with double caramel drizzle and Oreos on top" (my son picked that once and I almost said no), and his dad replies: "well, son, I can buy this for you, but I don't want to". My question, if I were the son, would be "WHY?!" Then I would scream, drop to the floor and throw the greatest tantrum I know how. Why would any loving father do that? What could he possibly get out of such a tease? If he wasn't willing, he should have left the little boy at home. There is no use calling the son's attention to things he - the father - is not willing to give, right?

So likewise, GOD is not a wicked father! If a human father knows what to do, how much more your heavenly Father? Matthew 7:11 reads: *"If you, then, though you are evil, know how to give good gifts to your children, how much more will your Father in heaven give good gifts to those who ask him!"* If humans can be nice to their children, GOD is infinitely nicer than we can understand.

When Jesus came down from the mountainside, large crowds followed him. A man with leprosy came and knelt before him and said, "Lord, if you are willing, you can make me clean." Jesus reached out his hand and touched the man. "I am willing," he said. "Be clean!" Immediately he was cleansed of his leprosy. (Matthew 8:1-3 NIV)

To be willing means to agree to do something out of the sheer kindness of one's heart, not because one is cajoled or compelled to. So, in other words, the man didn't want to pressure Jesus. He wanted it to be out of Jesus' own will, and not because he was being pestered. Here, you can see a perfect instance of someone who was convinced, beyond a shadow of a doubt, that Jesus could, but wanting to be sure Jesus was willing. This man understood that the ability to do something and the willingness to do the same are different things. He also understood that GOD is sovereign, and that He is not a genie. Willingness speaks to choice. GOD blessing us does not make him more or less of who He is; no, not at all. He is GOD regardless. He, however, does bless us because He chooses to do so. If GOD didn't do another thing in the whole earth, trust me when I say, it wouldn't change who He is. The fact that His chooses to bless us makes the gift even that more special. Glory! Hallelujah!! GOD is not a genie!!! His choice to relate to us in love is convicting, endearing, mind blowing and comforting all at the same time. What an amazing GOD we call Father!

Whenever I read scripture, especially in instances of good counsel being passed on, I personalize it. I read it as though Jesus is speaking to me. So, personalize the scripture above; personalize Jesus' response. Did you hear it? Jesus just said to you "I am willing". He is willing and that will never change. He was willing against all odds at the Garden of Gethsemane, when the thought of the cross weighed so heavily upon him that it almost crushed his physical heart. In spite of the cross, He was willing. He was willing with every skin-ripping stroke of the whip. He was willing as they mocked, pushed, and crowned Him with thorns. He was willing when they spat on Him. He was willing on that long and lonely walk up Golgotha. He kept His will with every excruciating nail driven into his hands, and then He was willing, yet still, to refrain from calling a legion of angels to black out the world, as they hung Him on the cross. He was willing as they laid Him out to die until He gave up the ghost. And He's still willing, now risen and seated at the right hand of GOD, The Father. He chooses to continue to be willing. There were more than enough chances to choose otherwise, but still He was willing to follow through on the plan for salvation and redemption. His choice was clear then and forever resounds now. His choice every day and in every situation is: "I am willing!"

GOD is always willing to do it for you.

Jesus is not only willing, He is willing to do it for *you*. Whatever it is you have heard Him say or do, or whatever He inspires in your heart to yearn after, He will do for you! When we think about Jesus dying on the cross for the world, the weight of what was laid on Him is amplified, as is the potency of His sacrifice. Maybe you can even comprehend the significance of Him dying for the whole world, — that in and of itself is beyond amazing — but when you think of the fact that He died for you, it shifts the focus from the multitude in the world, to just you. He died for me! What a remarkable sacrifice. We may not know all the world, but we know ourselves, and when we examine who we are — our pettiness, our myopia, even our best — it is glaring that if He can die for us, there is nothing He wouldn't be willing to do for us. So, if you have ever questioned His willingness to do for you, like I used to, please don't leave this page without settling that. Debunk that myth and embrace the truth in front of you today. For every request you have brought to Him, and every request you will ever bring to Him, know that, according to His word, He is forever willing. And for the reader who is saying: "you don't understand, Temi, my case is beyond terribly bad; my sins have so corrupted me than I know He wouldn't want the filth that I am". Especially to you, He says: "I'm willing, be clean!".

IT IS AVAILABLE

If I have one pet peeve (sure…I only have one…let's go with that for now), it's seeing the 'out of stock' message that some online stores display on clothes that are for sale. If it's out of stock, why display the item in the first place? I can understand searching for a particular item, and getting that message, but I just cannot fathom listing an item, knowing fully well that it is out of stock. You cannot hunger for what does not exist. Have you ever craved for some Whooties? I'm sure your answer was a no. I hope you didn't try looking that up in the dictionary, or better yet on the web? Don't bother, it doesn't exist. That was my point. You cannot crave what doesn't exist. If you desire it, it exists! If you desire it and somehow it's not a reality in this realm, it exists in GOD is the only reason you can desire or dream it in the first place. There are some things you can crave and be rest assured of their availability 'in stock': GOD's innumerable promises as laid out in scripture. There is not one promise that you will find 'out of stock'.

Whenever GOD speaks, He speaks from His own reality. In His reality, all things exist and they never run out. In Him, all things consist. The word consist talks of the content of a thing. This simply means, everything exists inside of GOD. And as He will never run out, no single promise, nor anything at all existing within Him, will ever run out. Know this for sure: It exists and it is available! And this answers the question many ask about the availability or possibility of their dreams in GOD.

GO ONE UP

Has He shown you something amazing? You can bet that there's so much more in His reality. More than you and I can ever comprehend. There is always further to go in GOD; He is truly inexhaustible. Just when you think you've gotten to the end of the rope, He extends it. GOD is eternal. He is boundless, timeless, and endless in all things. He's the only one that can truly expand our knowing. He takes men beyond what they think is impossible. If you yield to Him, He will show you things you have never seen before. The knowledge of GOD is a stepping stone, but we must not stop there. The knowledge of GOD is not meant for knowledge in and of itself. It's not sufficient to just know of God. It is meant to generate an appetite to know AND experience GOD. GOD wants us to know Him but also 'go one up' to experience Him in our everyday living. He reveals His reality to us so that we know what is possible in Him.

One of my favorite promises in scripture is in Luke 1:45 - *"Blessed is she who believed, for there will be a fulfillment of those things which were told her from the Lord".* I chew on this often. When I read that verse, I get two meanings, depending on how I process the word "for".

The word "for" in this verse can be understood as either a conjunction or a preposition. As a conjunction, it explains the reason behind something. A common synonym, in that case, is the word "because". For example: "I sing for joy" would be the same as "I sing because [of] joy". So, joy is what prompts my singing. Thus, you can read Luke 1:45 as: "Blessed is she who believed, *because* there will be a fulfillment of those things which were told her from the Lord". If that's the case, the core message of this verse is a fulfillment of what GOD has said no matter what. So, she is blessed who believes, rejoices in, and embraces it, even before it becomes a reality.

As a preposition, the word 'for' indicates the purpose or the intended goal of its preceding phrase or statement. So, a sentence like "I get an allowance for upkeep" would mean: I get an allowance for the purpose of my upkeep. So, my upkeep is dependent on my allowance, and because I have an allowance I can keep up myself. The focus here is the meaning it conveys: because I have an allowance my upkeep is settled. Thus, Luke 1:45 could be interpreted: "Blessed is she who believed, *and because she has believed* there will be a fulfillment of those things which were told her from the Lord".

Both of these interpretations are true! GOD is manifold, and so are His ways and His word. There are many folds of understanding in each word GOD speaks. Many layers of revelation within every single word.

> You will only begin to live
> it when you can believe it.

If what you believe determines what is fulfilled, you must be fully aware of what you believe. Believing carries with it an element of guarantee — being rest assured that what you have trusted, in faith, will not fail. Belief is the bridge between knowledge and experience. Believe GOD at what He says and you will experience what He has said. GOD is the only one worth believing. Believe what He says about you. You can't afford to believe anything less. Jesus said: {*My sheep hear my voice and the voice of another they will not follow].* You must not follow the voice of another by unconsciously taking their word over what Jesus has said concerning you. Don't shape your life, and who you are, on what other people say; especially not the contrary voices that come through your mind.

The mind can be a market place sometimes, you know. You can hear different people and voices in the market at the same time, but with focus and attention, you can tune out and hear the voice of the person with whom you are 'doing business'. Focus and pay attention to what GOD is saying. He's the source of truth. It doesn't matter who says what, or when or how they said it. Follow The Way, The Truth and The Life. And if you find that what you believe doesn't tally up with the word of GOD, like that man who came to Jesus, cry out to Jesus today: 'I believe! Please help my unbelief!'

Now that you know that GOD will only call your attention to what is available, that He can do all things, and that He will do anything for you, go one up and believe Him completely.

3

REFUSE EVERY DISTRACTION

There is something hopeful about a thing being 'new'. A new year, a new career, a new marriage, a new outlook — such things make us want to start afresh, creating new visions or goals for ourselves. Often, when establishing these new goals, we try to understand the things we ought to do to achieve the goals, but rarely do we seek out what <u>not</u> to do, to be sure we secure our goals. We must, however, understand that both lists are equally important — the to-do and the not-to-do lists.

There are always two sides to the coin of attainment — what you must do to attain and what you must stop doing so that you can attain. Same coin, two sides. To ensure a complete and continuous win, you must begin to pay attention to both sides. Don't just write and plan for what you need to do to attain; include a victory plan on what you must guard against and how you will guard against them so that your attainment can be whole and entire, wanting nothing!

It is costly, very costly, and especially draining, to concentrate only on what you need to do, while pushing the things you need to stop doing aside. If care is not taken, the person putting in the required effort to build their dreams may also stumble in the areas they need improvements, and tear down the very thing they have built; and they would be worse off than when they started out. GOD's promise to us is that our latter would be greater than the former; so, we must not give room for anything less. Remember, His desire is that you have a continuous and progressive win. Wisdom then dictates that we do both; embrace what we know we ought to do and refuse to indulge in the things we know we ought not to do, so that they don't become a liability to our own progress.

One of such things on the not-to-do list are distractions. Don't allow distractions.

•••••••

I mentioned earlier how I personalize scripture. This, certainly, is one to personalize.

> *So you, my son, be strong [constantly strengthened] and empowered in the grace that is [to be found only] in Christ Jesus. The things [the doctrine, the precepts, the admonitions, the sum of my ministry] which you have heard me teach*

[a]in the presence of many witnesses, entrust [as a treasure] to reliable and faithful men who will also be capable and qualified to teach others. Take with me your share of hardship [passing through the difficulties which you are called to endure], like a good soldier of Christ Jesus. No soldier in active service gets entangled in the [ordinary business] affairs of civilian life; [he avoids them] so that he may please the one who enlisted him to serve. And if anyone competes as an athlete [in competitive games], he is not crowned [with the wreath of victory] unless he competes according to the rules. The hard-working farmer [who labors to produce crops] ought to be the first to receive his share of the crops. Think over the things I am saying [grasp their application], for the Lord will grant you insight and understanding in everything. 2 Timothy 2:1-7 AMP

The scripture above warns that you must not get entangled in the business affairs of civilian life. That implies focus. Focus on the affairs of a soldier. This means that you must have the ability to distinguish between soldier business and civilian business. It also means that you must have the wisdom to react to either appropriately. To the one, you must focus; to the other, you must refuse. To refuse is to flat out reject a thing. It is to say or show that you are not willing to accept an offer. They often say, don't give everyone access to you; even so, don't give everything access to you. To win, you must hedge yourself against everything that seeks to work against your win. You must be conscious of what might be working against your intended course and position yourself in such a way that your course will not be altered. Life is certainly a mix of things, and while you may not be able to control all that comes your way, you can certainly control how you react to them. You have a choice whether to accept or refuse whatever comes.

THE WINDOW OF POSSIBILITY

Sight is one of the most engaged senses. It is used to perceive and decode the external world. Sight is especially important because you will only go as far as you can see, both physically and spiritually. It is what you see through GOD's eyes that you will dare to become. If you don't see anything, you will not become anything. This is why I am very particular about seeing *what GOD sees in you*. When you do, you get the assurance and permission you need, as well as the authority and audacity to actualize who you see through His eyes. Also, when you see yourself as He sees you, you will be amazed to find that GOD looks at you with love in His eyes. You must be convinced of this one thing today: GOD is bent on your win more than He is bent on keeping you at bay for your sins and shortcomings. Yes, you read that right. His highest desire is not to punish you; it is to love you and bring forth glory out of all your circumstances. But don't read that wrongly either, GOD still hates sin. That will not change. Sin hurts you and that hurts GOD. It will hurt any parent to see their child hurt themselves with gifts that ought to help them. And just as loving parents do not cast away their children because they make wrong choices, GOD does not desire to cast you away. All a loving parent wants is for their children to stop making wrong choices and begin making the right ones. So, if we as humans, evil in our natural state, know how to treat our children with compassion and love, how much more Pure Love Himself? GOD desires that no one perish but that all people will be saved and come to a knowledge of the truth. So, if any perish, they choose to perish on their own, not because GOD desires that they do. Again, I want to be clear, GOD wants more than anything that you are victorious at life.

> When you see yourself through GOD's eyes, you'll get the permission, authority and audacity to become what you see through His eyes.

•••••••

Faith is seeing! Your eyes of faith are windows through which you see what can be possible. When the bible says, *"faith is the assurance of things hoped for and the evidence of things not seen"*, it is really amplifying the fact that faith is the tangibility of something that was once intangible. While you may not yet see with your naked eyes the evidence of what you have hoped for, you must, in the very least, grab a hold of its essence with your spiritual eyes to even call it faith. You can't faith what you can't see in the spirit. Without seeing it in your spirit, that hope simply becomes wishful thinking. Faith is spiritual sight.

Let me also say this: you can't faith what you didn't hear in the spirit. Faith comes by hearing the word of GOD! When GOD speaks into your spirit, it comes with immediate conviction and a crispness you can't express. That's what happens when people say, "I don't know how but I just know it is done". When it is faith, you will not need to convince yourself about it; it comes with express conviction. It just hits you…boom! And immediately you have the evidence of the very thing. You may not see it with your natural eyes yet but your spirit man has gotten the picture, and that's all you need; because if you can faith it (see it in your spirit), you will see it with your naked eyes. Faith is a spirit thing.

"And the earth was without form, and void; and darkness was upon the face of the deep. And the Spirit of God moved upon the face of the waters." (Genesis 1:2 KJV)

Seeing is in two parts. First, we see in the spirit and we see in our physical reality. The truth is, everything starts without form and void…just like it was in the beginning. But as you keep speaking the word in faith, The Word — The presence of GOD (even the breath within you) – broods over the void and brings forth something out of nothing. When the spirit broods, something extraordinary is going on — GOD is depositing His manifold nature into the void; transferring His ability to become anything into the void so that a miracle can come out of it. The moment the void takes up shape in the spirit, it has become tangible and real in your spirit. And if it can take up form in your spirit, it will take up form in your reality.

Whatever you can dream up already exists in GOD or you

couldn't dream it in the first place. GOD does not begin to run around to create at the point of your request; He is the container that contains everything you could ever ask for or dream of. The bible says, "in Him all things consist", meaning all things exist inside Him. Whatever you ask for is already in existence even if you can't yet see it with your two eyes. That's why GOD can guarantee an immediate response if He chooses to do so. Everything you have ever needed in the past, everything you need now and all that you will ever need is ready and waiting to be claimed in Him. Your part is to claim it by the help of the Holy Spirit. Claim what is yours from the abundance that is GOD and then push it through into reality. *Push* until you see it play before your very eyes. Start no matter how small and push no matter how little, then watch your world take shape accordingly.

If it can take up form in your spirit, it will take up form in your reality.

I believe this is how GOD has made us partners with Him in the work of creation. He has created everything in the spirit and has given us the authority and access to pull it into our reality.

WHAT'S AT STAKE

If what you see in the spirit determines what translates into your reality, then you must refuse access to anything that seeks to skew your sight. Distractions skew the sight. Its important to note that distractions can be both physical and spiritual in nature. As a matter of fact physical distractions can have spiritual impact and spiritual distractions can have physical impact. This is why we must by all means necessary refuse every distraction. If a distraction succeeds in interrupting the process of creation, it may throw one off kilter long enough to stop the process or in the very least, prolong it. The purpose of distractions is to shift your focus from what is truly important to irrelevant things that seem urgent.

You must be direct and firm in refusing distractions; don't play with distractions at all. It's not a pet; it's very harmful to your destiny. While GOD intends that we win, we also must make choices that align us with that goal. The bible says shall two work together unless they agree? Your choices must agree with your desire, even GOD's desire, for you to achieve His ultimate goal in your life. One choice you must make is to create what GOD has called you to create and refuse all deviations. Note that to refuse and to resist are two different things. Refusing is light years ahead of resisting. When you resist a thing, it implies a struggle or some tug of war. After all is said and done, there is still a possibility to give in, even having fought the good fight. But when you refuse something, you stop dead it in its tracks, you kill its chances of getting to you, and you shut it down completely. To refuse implies a firm decision to turn away. To disallow it. To decline it. You are simply saying: No, thank you!

A BIG FAT "NO THANK YOU"

The rate at which we see and hear of nanny horrors on social media, makes me so glad to have a sister with a passion for kids. She runs a home daycare in our home where she has cared for my kids as well as others in our community. She cares for the boys with a care that rivals mine. With her, I don't have to worry about how my kids are being treated at all; I am always sure they are in loving, Christ-centered care all the time. She really has a thing for children and it shows. I won't be surprised if she ends up with a house filled with kids someday, because, when she doesn't go looking for them, they come looking for her and she enjoys every little interaction.

Little Owha was one of the boys she had in her care. He is such an adorable little boy. We all watched as he grew from trying to speak, to engaging adults in meaningful conversations, and it's a blessing to behold. One of the phrases little Owha used often was "No, Thank You", and I want to implore you to do the same. There are times he would take possession of the TV and prevent anyone from switching the channel. The thing is we only have one TV in our house and everyone is in competition for it. Sometimes, we would even offer little Owha cookies, or his favorite snack (popcorn), as a distraction from the television so others could get a chance to watch what they wanted. At first, the distractions worked, but soon enough they stopped working. Owha caught on quickly and would respond to all our attempts to distract him with a big fat "no, thank you". The first time he refused my yummy-distraction, I was shocked but soon came to understand that Little Owha was growing up and could now see beyond the distractions.

We can learn a whole lot from little Owha. It's okay that we once fell for those distractions. But like Owha, we too must grow up. As we grow, we will no longer fall for the same old tricks. Growth suggests that our senses are more developed and that we are better at using them in aiding our decisions. Simply put, we ought to be smarter and wiser over time. It's about time we start refusing distractions in our lives and meet them with a big, fat talk-to-the-hand-the-face-aint-listening "no, thank you!". That's how Owha did it. His little fingers propped up at an angle toward your face, firmly retorting "no, thank you". With that little gesture, Owha stopped many distractions in their tracks and carried along in his track. The best part is that he wouldn't even take his gaze off the television to respond to you.

SET JETS ON IT

Sometimes, all it takes is a second of distraction and we are knocked off our course. That's long enough to change entire destinies. This reminds me of a conversation I had recently with one of the families at RCCG Potter's House, the church where I'm Chief Servant (otherwise known as Pastor). I was visiting with the lovely couple, and while we were watching the news, we started talking about space and energy. The husband then recalled a meteor that was headed to earth some years ago. He explained that it was twenty times the size of earth and that it would have wiped out the whole earth if it indeed hit. As he explained the whole ordeal, he said something that stuck out to me. He said, "in the end, we set jets on it". He meant, the National Aeronautics and Space Administration (NASA) had to fire jets at it, in aims to alter its course. They knew the jets were no match for the meteor and that they would not stop or destroy it, but they weren't interested in that. All they wanted to do was shift its course, even if it's just a little bit — their aim was to distract it with a few punches.

Although the jets were no match, they were still able to distract the meteor. They succeeded in altering its course from earth's path. Most distractions are like that. They are not overpowering. In fact, distractions are usually no match for you. But, remember, their aim is not to destroy you; it is to distract you. Also understand that the distraction doesn't have to be for a lengthy period of time to take you off course. It only needs to have your attention, even if it's for a nanosecond.

A nanosecond is probably how long it took for the jets to be destroyed, but they accomplished their goal. And sometimes, it takes centuries to recover from a nanosecond's distraction – or in this particular case, two centuries, to be exact. According to my friend, the meteor will orbit around again in another 200 years or so. The lesson? Set your own jets against the distractions in your life. Learn to distract your distractors so they don't consume you.

••••••••

Distractions can come from any angle or anyone. Sometimes, it comes from loved ones, foes, friends, and anyone else in between. In the case of loved ones, most of the time, they don't even realize they are distracting you in moments that they do. They are genuinely only trying to protect you. A perfect example is the case of Jesus and Peter. After Jesus told Peter the awesome, but certainly, bone-chilling plan of salvation, Peter said in response *"be it far from you Lord"*. He responded ignorantly, but certainly filled with love and care for his master. He couldn't understand how such a contradiction (which is what he thought it to be) could be the plan; and how or why Jesus would be so welcoming of such. Thank GOD Jesus was confident about His calling. Can you just imagine if that were you? Imagine how indecisive you would immediately become. Imagine how quick we are to waver at GOD's word when loved ones see or say the contrary? Imagine telling a beloved friend about GOD's intended purpose for you and they advise like Peter did. We might be quick to agree with them and miss out on the very purpose for our lives. I have said it many times in my life, and I'll say it again and again: Thank GOD for Jesus! Thank GOD for the example He is to us.

A NOLLYWOOD GIFT

Some months ago, I watched an interesting Nollywood movie. Nollywood is the Nigerian movie industry, similar to Hollywood here in the United States. I rarely watch television but when I do, it would most likely be for a movie. There I was on that great night. My husband called out to me "this is a must watch" he said. He sounded very convincing, so I sat down to watch with him. Movies are extremely rare for him, but he had seen this one and thought to share it with me. "Don't miss a thing," he stressed, as I sat down with full concentration. Boy! That movie was gift to my world! The sad part is that didn't catch the title. It was rolling already when I started watching and I didn't realize the impact it had on me until the next day. We have searched for that movie ever since then with no luck.

Although, I can't share the whole movie, because I'm sure some of you will stumble on it like I did and I don't want to be a spoiler, I will share a few things. The movie was about an aggressively, assertive woman with a foul tongue. She was not one to suffer anything lightly; good, bad or ugly…she kicked back against everything. The woman had been going through some hardship in her life: searching for a job for some time, and was fed up with each unsuccessful interview. She was just frustrated about life and how things were working against her. So, she responded to life in that same spirit.

Shortly into the movie, she had a dream in which a woman, whose name was Wealth, called out to her and promised to make her wealthy. Wealth shared the secrets of obtaining wealth with her and instructed her to do only one thing to become wealthy. Wealth gave her some new clothes to wear and the task laid upon her was simple: wear the clothes home. Wealth instructed her firmly: "Do not lose these clothes". This woman was very confident that she wouldn't lose the clothes because she was going to be wearing them on her person. She was also especially confident because her house was close by, according to the details of the dream.

As she walked home, excited about all that had happened — her breakthrough had finally come — she met a man on the way; his name, Humiliation. When Humiliation saw her, he did what he knew to do best — cause humiliation. She felt insulted and aggravated, and before you knew it, she who suffered nothing lightly, took off her clothes and was ready to rumble. To my surprise, as soon as she took her clothes off, Humiliation cowered down. His countenance suddenly changed. He even began to plead with her. He apologized for all he had said to her and claimed he was mistaken. She was calmed by his apologies, but when she reached for her clothes, they were gone! Her wealth — her breakthrough — as implied by the dream, had vanished. For a second's distraction, she lost her balance and had now lost everything she had dreamt of. You will have to watch the movie for the rest of the storyline but that dream spoke volumes to me.

On the road to victory, you must refuse every distraction! Don't let the small things bother you and don't let the big ones capture your mind. On the road to live out the fullness within you, you can't afford to be distracted — not even for a second. Every distraction steals your focus; it hampers the quality and momentum of your focus. Distraction is adversity against your vision; they shift what you see and what you focus on. And in that little shift, a lot can be lost. Humiliation, in that story, was nothing but a distraction. If only she knew to refuse him and keep on her path.

Distractions are only doing what they were created to do: distract. Humiliation was flourishing in his own purpose; he was in his own element, attaining his own goal. It's just unfortunate, that his goal was opposed to hers. Your goal is to flourish in your own element. You must keep focus and not let other things that are focused on their own mission, make you lose out on yours. Humiliation had a job and it was to humiliate, and he was going to do his job to the best of his abilities. She also had a job, to get home with her clothes; she ought to have done hers also to the best of her abilities. In her case, getting home with her clothes required focus and humility. She didn't need to say a word to him, but she couldn't get past own her pride. Humility is always the cure for humiliation. Indeed, he that is down needs fear no fall at all; he has already made himself as nothing so calling him nothing means nothing to him.

On the road to victory, don't
let the small things bother
you and don't let the big
ones capture your mind.

THE QUALITY ASSURANCE TEAM

Many are the things that can easily distract and lead us on a tangent, but we must prove firm on our course, no matter what. Honestly, distractions are not really against you; they are simply a part of the quality assurance team. The quality assurance team proves you. Their job is to ensure you are really built for what you're supposed to do. How GOD-purpose-driven tough are you? The quality assurance team is there to prove how durable you are in that purpose. They prove whether what they have heard GOD say about you is really true. Refuse every distraction and they'll prove God's purpose perfected in you.

In a concept called Software Development Life Cycle (SDLC), once developers build a system and all the coding is done, the system is handed over to the quality assurance team for proofing. In the proofing stage (also known as testing), testers throw different scenarios at the system with an aim to 'break' it — expose weaknesses and loopholes in its functionality. It is important to note that the quality of that software is directly proportional to the quality of scenarios tested in attempts to prove it. And when a software goes through all those scenarios, and is found tested and true to its intended build, then it's complete and ready for use.

Distractions are part of the quality assurance team of your life. And as it is in SDLC, the different scenarios and testers that come your way will expose your weaknesses and the loopholes that are in your own build. You must not shy away from them. We'll talk about weakness in a later chapter, but it's important to know that when you go through that process, you become better at what you were created for.

KNOW YOUR CUSTOMER

KYC is a federal regulation in the United States of America that demands that businesses identify and verify their customers. These days, it's an important part of any business transaction. That's why most companies ask for your identification and verify your information as best they can in the course of doing business with you.

KYC is essential to our lives too. We must vet the 'customers' we do business with. We must be able to identify them all, proceed with those we wish to do business with and decline the ones we shouldn't have dealings with. Identifying them is the first step to refusing and overcoming them. Know your customers and know your distractors!

There are different types of distractions. Some are obvious, others are subtle. Some are potent, others are weak. Whichever kind they are, we must be able to identify them so that we can overcome them. Here are a few:

Offenses are one of the most common, most potent, and most effective distractions. They always happen. And when they do, we usually fall headlong, tumbling down in them long before we ever see them as distractions. As long as we have interactions and relationships with other people, we cannot prevent offenses from occurring. The thing with offenses is that they can come from anyone, including you. As strange as it sounds, it's the reality for many. And when you are offended or angry with yourself, who can convince you to let go but yourself? Sounds like a mind twister, huh? As long as there are relationships, there will be offenses. You can even find offenses if you live on a deserted island alone. Need proof? The American epic survival drama with Tom Hanks, *Cast Away*, proves my point. If you haven't watched the movie, go ahead and treat yourself to it. I must say it's an oldie, but goodie. On an uninhabited island, where he finds himself alone, due to a plane crash, Tom Hanks, who plays Chuck Noland, was offended with his make shift soccer ball friend. Believe me, if Chuck can get offended with a ball, you can get offended by any and everyone, including yourself.

Even if you can control yourself and ensure offenses don't come from you toward others, you can't control others and what comes from them. So, the task you are faced with is how you deal with offenses once it's dished out. What must you do? You must actively guard against offenses, if we're to attain our goals and secure our win. We must consciously and actively outwit them, otherwise they would derail us for as long as you latch on to them. When we are focused on offenses we certainly can't focus on much else.

Guilt is another one of those universal distractors. For every wrong choice we make, guilt is bound to come knocking. But what you do with it is what makes or breaks you. The negative response to guilt is to sit and wallow in it. The more appropriate response to guilt is turning from your current course and taking another route. Guilt was designed as an alert to warn you when you are going down the wrong path. We must acknowledge guilt, but be quick to find its root cause and turn to go the direction of GOD.

Sin is another one of those grave distractions but there's a whole chapter on that; just keep reading. And there are others but you must do the homework on what easily besets you and consciously choose against them.

DEALING WITH DISTRACTION

When you identify a distractor, you don't deal gently with it. It's not the time for negotiations or diplomacy. It's not the time to resist. It's time to flee. There is a time for everything, and in the face of a besetting distractor, act immediately. Drastic situations call for drastic measures. The bible says if your eyes cause you to err, pluck it out (figuratively speaking, that is). Pluck out that thing immediately.

I found a subtle distraction in my life. I didn't realize it quick enough, but as soon as I did, GOD inspired a solution to nip it in the bud. Social media was a huge distraction for me. It was tricky dealing with this particular distraction because a part of my work in the ministry is done through social networks. An online presence in this age is essential for success. Social media helps you keep in touch with those in your world, also giving one the ability to reach broader audiences, all at a click of a button. It's an amazing tool when used correctly. But it had become my distraction.

It was slowly knocking me off course. I was telling myself I needed to be on there so much because I was helping and engaging people all over the world. There is nothing wrong with that but you ought to know something's not right if you spend most of your day on social media whiling away your time. When do you have time to live life, birth your dreams, sharpen yourself, focus on GOD, etc.? I knew it was a big problem when the first thing I wanted to do when I woke up was check and post on social media. It had begun to take the place of hearing GOD when I wake up. And before I realized it, I found myself wasting hours just scrolling up and down my timeline. Many days, I would refresh and then scroll up and down again. I'd read and reread the same posts over and over like someone in a trance. When I first identified the problem, I didn't do anything about it. I didn't know what to do because it had almost become a reflex action. Whenever I was with my phone, even when my intention was to not go on a social network, I would find myself there. I had to cut it off. I had to cut off the constant and unproductive browsing. I knew I had to cut it off, or it would cut me off.

So, I talked to GOD about it and as an answer to my prayers, He inspired my heart to recondition the stimulus. It brought to mind something I learnt in science many years ago: conditioning. There are three types of conditioning, one of which applies here. The applicable one is called classical conditioning. The theory is that if a neutral stimulus is paired with a stimulus that already evokes a reflex response, then eventually the new stimulus will by itself evoke the response without needing the old stimulus. I'm not sure scholars would agree that my thumb clicks are stimuli, but I hope this illustration helps you understand what GOD inspired me to do. The Lord instructed me to place the social media icons into a group and place them on the last page of apps away from other apps, preventing easy access. He also instructed me to place my bible apps in the exact spots where the social media icons once resided on my phone. So that whenever the thumb memory kicks in, I would find myself in the bible rather than where I didn't want to be. This may sound too simple, but it worked for me.

The solution to these distractions doesn't have to be drastic or elaborate; they can be as simple as reconditioning a habit or as small as jets deflecting a huge meteor. The size of the distraction does not determine the size of the solution. But it requires wisdom to fix it. I didn't have the wisdom to help myself, so I asked The One who did. Lacking wisdom doesn't mean one is dumb. Remaining without wisdom because you don't want to feel dumb is what makes one truly dumb. *"If any of you lack wisdom, let him ask of GOD, that gives to all men liberally, and without reproach, and it will be given to him,"* says the Lord.

I hope this chapter has helped you see the role of distraction. It fulfills its part in existence and you have must fight hard against it to fulfill your part in existence, even your destiny. You don't need to do it the exact way I did because what might have worked for me might not work for you. However, seek GOD to help you conquer every distraction and/or addiction in your life. For with GOD, you can and will refuse all distractions.

4

REFUSE EVERY EXCUSE

GOD never misses a teachable moment. Whether it be in the middle of a heated argument, or while correcting your kids, or in solemn thought, GOD is ever speaking and ever teaching. Those who are attentive will hear Him always. It especially warms my heart when I read in a book or hear from another's mouth, the jaw dropping truths GOD taught me in the secret of our communion. And it truly blows my mind when a friend texts me, or I come across a stranger's post on social media about the same thing GOD whispered to my hearing, at about the same time. In moments like that, I am convinced that while GOD can speak to us individually and tailors His wisdom to our situation or circumstance, He can also speak to us as a teacher would in a classroom, and every student would hear Him at the same time.

GOD enjoys conversations with us; that's why He talks all the time. He doesn't only speak in certain places or situations, He is always eager to bring us into the knowledge of His perfect will and has no desire to keep us in the dark about anything at all. Although most people seem to hear GOD when they are quiet, note that you can hear GOD in any place, at any time, and in the middle of anything. GOD can leverage any situation to speak to you or teach you the indelible. GOD speaks to me a lot in day to day interactions with my kids.

I am convinced that kids are channels through which GOD teaches their parents. You would think it's the other way around, but GOD teaches them through us as much as He teaches us through them. For me, it happens right in the heat of the moment: when I am passionately conveying a truth, in an attempt to set them straight. I'd simply hear that still small voice say: "you've got it", or, my personal favorite, "that's exactly how I feel when you don't listen". His voice jolts and interrupts my thoughts, causing me to abandon my course of action. My kids often wonder what the sudden shift is all about. They probably just think I'm weird. But I know in due time the acorn will become a tree, and they too will experience this phenomenon. Hopefully, they'd rethink that opinion.

THE FIG TREE

One day Jesus was walking by a fig tree and reached for its fruits. He found out as He searched for fruit on the tree that there was none. He was upset and cursed the tree. Interestingly, it was recorded that it wasn't the season for figs yet. At first, I was confused as to why Jesus would curse a tree that wasn't producing in a season it wasn't meant to. It's one thing if it were the season for figs and the tree hadn't produced. So why would Jesus curse a tree that seems to be growing according to its — shall I say — ordained life cycle? That seemed strange to me. But one day, it hit me: there are no good enough reasons to refuse GOD access to your fruits. It doesn't matter whether it's in or out of season; when GOD comes knocking you must display the wonder He put in you. No excuses.

Think about it. Do you think the creator of seasons and times did not know what season it was? Should it surprise the knower of all things that it wasn't the season for figs yet? Surely, He knew, and yet, he beckoned on the tree for fruits. That's because when GOD comes into a situation, everything changes. Out of season suddenly becomes in season, at His command. He is the constant that changes all things and disrupts the norm, if and how He pleases. Natural laws ain't got nothing on Him. Seasonal cycles don't come close. He created them and can tweak them all as He wishes.

> There are no good
> reasons to refuse GOD
> access to your fruits.

A similar thing happened at the wedding in Canaan. Mary — Jesus' mom — came to Him with a report that the wine at the wedding had run out. She wanted Him to do something about it and He responded saying, "*...my time has not yet come*". But He then went on and turned water in six stone water pots, each holding about 20 - 30 gallons of water, into wine. I ask myself this: it wasn't His time, yet and He brought forth about 150 gallons of wine. What would have happened if it was His time? Would He have turned all the waters in the world into wine?

It's unfortunate that no other character in the Bible ran out of wine at the peak of Jesus' ministry, else we would have found out. But the real question to dote on is this: how come He acted though "his time hadn't yet come"? I believe He was sensitive to the Holy Spirit, and recognized that The Father had created a situation in order to reveal Himself. I honestly believe if Jesus had done nothing, the guests at the wedding would have been just fine. They might have complained a little bit but they would have gotten over it in time, as they've probably done at other weddings in the past. It definitely wasn't a do or die affair. So, what moved Christ to take action though it wasn't His time yet? The same reason that should have compelled the fig tree to produce fruit. It was an opportunity to reveal GOD. When GOD creates a moment in time to reveal Himself, we have no good excuse to fall behind; we must go ahead to prove Him. Imagine what the story would have been if that fig tree produced, even though it wasn't the season for figs. It would have been a wonder; an immediate proof of GOD, in that instant. Who knows... the people could have set up an altar there, as is the custom in some cases where the supernatural happens.

We also must never get stuck on whether it's our season to

produce or not. We must never deny GOD the wonder He intends to express through our lives. In every situation, in which GOD intends to reveal Himself, we must rise to the occasion as Jesus did. Whatever your reason for why you think you cannot or should not, it will always pale in comparison to the potential wrapped up in your obedience. No excuses can justify suppressing or disobeying GOD's command. The simple gesture (when Jesus stretched His hands) should have compelled that fig tree to yield fruit. No excuses. Don't stall at the life-giving word of GOD; do not be idle at His command. Remember, His thoughts towards you are thoughts to grant you an expected end — a winning existence. Simply jump at the word and see where it leads. Jump to produce at His every word! You can be sure it will lead to a miracle.

We must never deny GOD
the wonder He intends to
express through our lives.

•••••••

Jesus also leveraged the drying up of this tree as a teachable moment. He taught His disciples saying: *"I tell you the truth, if you have faith and don't doubt, you can do things like this and much more. You can even say to this mountain, 'May you be lifted up and thrown into the sea,' and it will happen."*

The verse above teaches us what it truly takes to create a miracle. Faith is a requirement to accomplish anything but there's another piece to it: not doubting. We must aid our faith by eliminating the doubt that rises in our hearts. If faith was enough, Jesus would have simply said 'have faith and the mountain will move'. But as He taught us, faith cannot have its perfect work without dealing with doubt, especially because we can have faith, and still doubt. Doubt and faith are like fear and courage; they are not mutually exclusive as we often think. Just as courage is not the absence of fear, but a conscious choice to be strong and carry on in spite of fear, so is faith's relationship with doubt. It is not the absence of doubt; it is simply the conscious choice of assured hope over whatever may be whispered into your heart to the contrary. It is consciously choosing that doubt will not prevail.

FAITH ALWAYS WINS

My career has been one great adventure, I must say. While most people stick to one passion within a particular discipline, I have been privileged to contribute to many different disciplines in the course of my career. I've come to understand that every role I played in these various fields are linked to the ability to fully express all that's within me, even as I fulfill my purpose now. Just to give you an idea, I have been a Research Chemist at a Pharmaceutical Company, a telemarketer, salesperson, a banker, a biochemist and more recently, the Vice President of Analysis in technology at a bank. I guess you can say the science of every art intrigues me. Whether it is the chemical reaction between substances, the intrinsic nature of living organisms, investments and money, or technology and its different aspects; one thing is sure: I have many passions and I have been afforded the opportunities to explore some of them. And I'm still exploring.

A lot of people ask me how I did that — switch between completely unrelated fields. Honestly, I'll say with diligence, willingness and most importantly, GOD, all things are possible. Whenever I was making any drastic switch between fields, I held on to this fact without compromise: I am the seed of my Father and His character is in me. My Father is omniscient which means He knows all things. As His child, I have the capacity to learn anything I need to know to excel in whatever my endeavors are. We truly can become all things to all men if we so desire and more importantly if we let GOD work it out in us. With a mule-like resolve to stop excuses from stopping you and an understanding that GOD is indeed your very present help, you are possible — you and every dream in you. There is no height you cannot reach if you refuse the excuses that try to waylay you. The truth is nothing in life will just fall on your lap, not even the things that heaven has ordained for you. Remember the Quality Assurance team is always at work, testing and proving as they should. You must desire it more than you choose the excuses in your head. There is absolutely nothing you can't do because you are the seed of The Father.

When I was making my last career move, GOD gave me a word. He said: "I will make room for you". That should have secured me firmly, right? I mean, GOD spoke! But still, I battled doubt in my heart. At that time, I had been working in a bank for some years. Right when the financial bubble burst in 2008, and the economy was at its worst, I was in the financial industry helping people plan their money. Actually, my husband and I were both in the financial industry at that time. The whole thing reminds me of the story of Moses, who was hidden by GOD in the very house of the king who had ordered the killing of children his age throughout the nation of Egypt. Forgive me for drawing similarities between the ethics displayed by the financial industry and Pharaoh's brutality, but like Moses, my husband and I were securely hidden in the bull's eye of the economic crisis of 2008. If I must be honest with you, I never saw it like that until writing out these words. I disliked every moment of the three years I was there, and a significant amount of time was spent every day trying to get out of it.

However, it soon became clear that GOD wanted me hidden for a little while. When I finally got the release to venture out, GOD gave me a series of assuring promises, of which "I will make room for you" was the first. But with every assuring word came challenges that threw doubt my way. You would think it got easier with each transition, having gone through many industry switches like that in the past. But with each one, the battle seemed to intensify. Change is never comfortable. But through it all, GOD taught me not to flinch at His promises, no matter how thick the fog of doubt became.

One thing we can count on, if we don't flinch, is faith always wins. But I have noticed that whenever we find faith and doubt present in us at the same time, we tend to throw our faith out the window. After all, it must not be faith if we are doubting, right? That's really not the case. I have found that most of the time, the presence of doubt causes us to question if we heard GOD at all in the first place. But consider this: when you are trusting GOD for what is impossible to man, it's okay if you — man — find yourself in doubt. It's normal! It happens to everyone. There is nothing wrong with your faith. The trick is to beef it up, not discard it. Recalibrate your thoughts to faith, leaving out the doubt. Don't throw away your faith because doubt is present. Throw away your doubts because faith is present. Trade with GOD — your doubts for His rest.

> Don't throw away your faith
> because doubt is present.
> Throw away your doubts
> because faith is present.

DEFY THE ODDS

Winners are bold. Boldness is one of their major strengths. Winners are also daring; they dare to dare. Daniel 11:32 says: *"The people that know their GOD will be strong and do exploits"*. One of my friends recently appended that verse for clarity. She said, '... they do exploits, not fold arms'.

When we talk of exploits, that's not something you stumble upon. Exploits require great resolve, and a stubborn determination. They are not for the faint hearted. You cannot fold your arms and expect to do exploits. You must act boldly. You must be brave. Exploits do not happen by idle hands. When I think of people who performed exploits, I think of the likes of Daniel, Gideon, Paul, Peter, and others through whom the power of GOD was revealed to defy odds — simply because they dared to know their GOD and who they were in Him. We were created to defy odds! That's the original intent of His design. That's why there will always be an innate drive prompting you to break barriers and push past the ordinary. This is a part of everyone's spiritual DNA. But only a few push through to actualization.

When I think of exploits, I particularly reflect on the record of David conquering Goliath:

"David left his things with the keeper of supplies and hurried out to the ranks to greet his brothers. As he was talking with them, Goliath, the Philistine champion from Gath, came out from the Philistine ranks. Then David heard him shout his usual taunt to the army of Israel (Why are you all coming out to fight?" he called. "I am the Philistine champion, but you are only the servants of Saul. Choose one man to come down here and fight me! If he kills me, then we will be your slaves. But if I kill him, you will be our slaves! I defy the armies of Israel today! Send me a man who will fight me!") .... David replied to the Philistine, "You come to me with sword, spear, and javelin, but I come to you in the name of the Lord of Heaven's Armies—the God of the armies of Israel, whom you have defied. Today the Lord will conquer

you, and I will kill you and cut off your head. And then I will give the dead bodies of your men to the birds and wild animals, and the whole world will know that there is a God in Israel! And everyone assembled here will know that the Lord rescues his people, but not with sword and spear. This is the Lord's battle, and he will give you to us!" As Goliath moved closer to attack, David quickly ran out to meet him. Reaching into his shepherd's bag and taking out a stone, he hurled it with his sling and hit the Philistine in the forehead. The stone sank in, and Goliath stumbled and fell face down on the ground. So, David triumphed over the Philistine with only a sling and a stone, for he had no sword. Then David ran over and pulled Goliath's sword from its sheath. David used it to kill him and cut off his head." (1 Samuel 17:20-51 NLT)

One thing David did not have that day, as the army of GOD (Israel) faced Goliath and the Philistine army, were excuses. Rather, he found for himself reasons to be bold, and encouraged himself to dare. Within that unskilled, ruddy young man that day were no such reasons as to why He shouldn't or couldn't face Goliath. Even if he had some, we'd never know because he effectively parked them aside and went on with courage. And when others — the king and his brothers — brought up great excuses on his behalf, He turned them down. "No, thank you" He said. "This one's on GOD". This is what you also must do to accomplish exploits: refuse excuses. You must embolden and encourage yourself, even when no one is around to encourage you. Trust in the Lord your GOD and begin to live from the victory that has already been won for you.

If you were there, you probably would have placed your bet on Goliath. He looked the part and his resume was quite impressive. For starters, it included 'giant' and David was certainly not one. Goliath was a trained warrior skilled in his art; David was just a little shepherd boy. The Philistines were so sure they had bagged this battle, they couldn't see any other outcome. Israel had accepted defeat, and were so sure of David's impending death at the hands of the giant. He went out to Goliath with no sword, no shield, no back up — nothing. All the odds, as they knew it, were simply against him in this battle. But in the twinkling of an eye, everything changed. GOD showed up on the scene and everyone marveled at what happened next. When GOD shows up, those odds that were supposedly against you suddenly turn in your favor. With a single shot off a sling, David defied them all and brought down the giant warrior of the Philistine army as well as that giant warrior called doubt that was at the forefront of everybody's mind. The bible says, with GOD all things are possible. This also implies that without GOD, nothing is possible. He is the determining factor; He is the Determinator. David was with GOD and Goliath was not, and that made all the difference. I don't doubt the physical odds against you are stacked miles high. I don't even doubt they may look like giants before your little frame. But you must never lose sight of who you're with. Who you're with matters a lot.

JESUS UNDERSTANDS; DO YOU?

Excuses cost you more than they buy you.

As soon as those words hit my heart, I knew they were beyond me. Such profoundness can only be released by GOD. Excuses will surely cost you more than they can ever buy you. You engage in them with the hope that they'll buy you an opportunity to get ahead. But in reality, they only reduce you. Excuses are the reasons we put forth to pacify ourselves for not doing what we ought to do when we ought to do them. They are reasons we give ourselves to permit a 'less than' existence and be okay with it. They are reasons we convince ourselves to disobey GOD's commands. If only we knew that the 'side effects' of excuses surpass their enticement, and are not worth us trading our victory for.

Excuses tone down the quality of GOD's own glory in your life. They alter the flavor of your life. I hear a lot of people give excuses like "Jesus understands". Yes, He absolutely does! He is very familiar with our infirmities and knows too well our frailty. But He also understands the potential of His immeasurable, un-limited, and overwhelmingly great power at work within us. He understands this all too well. That's why He will not settle for anything less for us. It's the same dilemma a parent has, knowing the potential of their child. They refuse to settle for just mediocre from the child. If you must win, and win fully in this season, you will need to do away with excuses.

GOD lives within you. He died so He can live inside you.

Now, He doesn't only want to stay inside you, He wants it all: to live inside you, be with you, be by your side, and be over you as Lord. The bible says out of your belly will flow rivers of living waters. Jesus is that living water, and He wants to flow out of you as well. Many people are satisfied just having GOD live on the inside and seek to make a pond of Him rather than an ever-flowing river. Now that He's made His way inside, He wants more than anything else to flow out. He doesn't want to be shut in. GOD resides inside us so we can become one with Him and be empowered by Him. And He seeks to flow out so you can become proof of Him. Most assuredly, Jesus does understand, but do you? Do you understand who you are in Him? Do you understand the presence that powers you up, and seeks to do exceedingly great things through you? Do you understand what is at stake with your excuses? I presume not. I didn't too...until the Lord was gracious to open my eyes to it.

Excuses cost you more than they buy you.

If you truly understood, you would be weary of the trade-offs you make. I believe if everyone is given a fair chance to make well informed decisions, we would all choose well. If all the chips involved are plain and open on the table, I am confident that every man will make the right choice in every situation. Maybe my confidence is too optimistic, but I'd rather that than pessimism.

However, the decision-making process becomes complex because we don't always have a full picture of our situations. This is where our dependency on GOD ought to be amplified. GOD already warned us not to lean on our own understanding, but many of us still do. And if we want to be honest with ourselves, that's part of the problem: that box of understanding we call a mindset. The core of what we house there is based on our own knowledge. But what knowledge does man have? Let's go to the root of the matter.

> *Then the LORD God formed the man from the dust of the ground. He breathed the breath of life into the man's nostrils, and the man became a living person. Then the LORD God planted a garden in Eden in the east, and there he placed the man he had made. The LORD God made all sorts of trees grow up from the ground—trees that were beautiful and that produced delicious fruit. In the middle of the garden he placed the tree of life and the tree of the knowledge of good and evil…. The LORD God placed the man in the Garden of Eden to tend and watch over it. But the LORD God warned him, "You may freely eat the fruit of every tree in the garden— except the tree of the knowledge of good and evil. If you eat its fruit, you are sure to die." (Genesis 2:7-9, 15-17 NLT).*

Of all the plants and trees GOD created, He placed two special trees in the middle of the Garden of Eden: the tree of life and the tree of knowledge of good and evil. The tree of knowledge of good and evil could have otherwise been called the tree of death because GOD warned that man would surely die if he eats of it. GOD's instructions were simple: man could eat of any other tree with no restrictions. He could eat of the tree of life with no reservations. But never should he eat of the tree of the knowledge of good and evil. The two trees were opposites: one was life and the other was death. So, if in the one, death is found in the knowledge of good and evil, what then was in the tree of life? No knowledge or the lack of understanding of good and evil? And that brings me to another question: If man did not know good or evil, what did he know? What did man, in the perfected state, understand?

The answer to that question revolutionized my understanding. All man knew was GOD! That, in itself, proves why GOD didn't want man having any other type of knowledge. But the serpent beguiled Eve, and she did eat of the forbidden tree, and proceeded to give it to her husband. Adam. So, if the knowledge of good and evil is death, then we have only deepened our stake and dug our heel deeper into the very thing GOD didn't want us to have in the first place. The knowledge we ought to have is far greater than the knowledge of good and evil. There is more to knowledge than just being able to understand and differentiate what is good and what is evil, or better still, being able to decide to do good or evil. A man filled with knowledge of good is great and commendable, but certainly incomparable to a man filled with GOD.

Life, unfortunately, is not simply two dimensional: positive and negative, life and death, good and bad, north and south, length and breath. There are other dimensions, known and unknown to man. Life is not always black or white. In reality, we spend most of our time living in the gray. But even in the gray, we still need to choose to win! I'll share an illustration to help explain. Imagine you are in a restaurant and there is a baby in a car seat on the table next to you. While the parents were distracted, you noticed the car seat, with the baby, about to fall off the table. Would you try to save the baby? I'm sure 99.9% of people would say yes (I'll leave the 0.1% for those who would not answer and read on before they think about it). For those that answered yes, would you consider yourself a hero? I'm sure you're feeling confident and even proud of your response right now, as I was when initially asked. Now, let's fast forward 30 years. Would you still think you did a good thing if you found out that the baby you saved many years ago grew up to be a serial killer? For those who might still answer yes, I'll add one extra level of complication: what if they were planning to kill you? I don't mean to paint a gory picture, but it's important to help drive home the point. Again, I'm sure 99.9% of you would now rethink your original saving move, wouldn't you? This example is really not a case study on what is right or wrong to do. It just goes to prove that good or evil is relative and not two-dimensional. Time and eternity has a part to play in making sound decisions. That's why we cannot but fully rely on GOD! While we may have a firm grasp of handling a two-dimensional world, He knows all the dimensions and makes decisions from a truly holistic view that we can't predict. But He is willing to share His view of the grand scheme of things with us, if we let Him.

••••••••

> A man filled with good is
> great and commendable,
> but he is incomparable to
> the man filled with GOD.

The other part of the issue is we don't take the time to truly search things out. On the first day of 2017, which happened to be a Sunday, a very dear aunt forwarded me a viral message going around the social networks. She had received it like thousands of others and simply passed it on. The message stated that every month-date combo which were numerical doubles in the year would all be Sundays. So 1/1/2017, 2/2/2017, 3/3/2017…and so on would be Sundays. At first I was amazed, I believed it. But then I thought how could that be? So, I pulled out my calendar and the proof was there; it was a lie! But thousands, at the time I saw it, had viewed it and thought it worth sharing with others. I couldn't share it because I found out it was inaccurate. Some excuses are like that: they were passed on to us, and we just believed them. We didn't bother to seek out the truth, neither did the people who passed it on to us, and those who passed it to them. The chain is unending.

It is also important to know that excuses are based on fear. But fear is nothing but shadows. Have you ever panicked when you saw a scary shadow? Your mind plays tricks on you about what it is and how it's going to get you. You rush as quickly as you can to switch on the light so you get a better chance to fight it off, then you see that it was just a little brooch on your dresser, with feathers on it! That happened to me some years ago, and it taught me a great lesson on fear. Fear is a shadow. It is not real. I guess that's why some people say F.E.A.R is: False Evidence Appearing Real. Also, have you ever noticed that no matter how scary the shadow looks on the wall, it never comes near you? The truth is: shadows can't touch you. They can't walk, can't talk, can't do anything. Their power is in scaring you; nothing more. We must not give in to the shadows, no matter what they look like. Honestly, I can't even begin to describe what I thought I saw in the shadows that day. But the bible says GOD has not given us the "spirit of fear" but one of boldness and soundness of mind. GOD has not given us the spirit of excuses either.

When you want to nourish a tree, you go to the roots. The same is true when you want to uproot it. To uproot your excuses, you must find the fears they are rooted in. Switch on the light! Examine those thoughts in the light of GOD's word and see if the shadows can hold up without the cloak of darkness — the lies. Once you have identified the root, you must move it out of place. I did that with the brooch. Once I saw the little thing on my dresser, I moved it into the drawer where it belongs, tucked away from the light from my laptop that caused the scary shadow. Obviously, my eyes were playing tricks on me that day.

WHAT'S AT STAKE?

I have always thought flavor was about taste until I read an article that clarified it as a combination of taste and smell. I was so shocked that I rushed to my dictionary to verify it. I was pleasantly amazed. It's true: flavor is a combination of taste and smell.

Ever thought you knew the meaning of a word and then found that you had been misusing it the whole time? Well, this doesn't qualify as a total misuse; after all, taste is still part of the definition. But I certainly never used it with respect to its true meaning prior to that day. Flavor is about savoring food and experiencing the pleasure the food brings, not just to the body, but to the soul. It's through flavor that food attempts to touch the soul and release a satisfaction that's beyond a full stomach.

I rely on my sense of smell a lot when cooking. Interestingly, I rarely taste my food while cooking. I don't know why or when this started but that's how I cook. I can tell if I'm on the right track simply by the aroma. It somehow tells me if the ingredients are well balanced. Hence, without tasting, I can tell whether the meal I'm preparing is good or not. However, there's one thing I've not been able to detect by smell: salt. So, whenever the salt content is insufficient (or outright missing) in a dish, I usually find out with everyone else at the dinner table.

It's amazing how every ingredient in the dish doesn't quite harmonize on the palette until salt is present. It is even more amazing that you only require a little bit to make great impact. Salt is a binder, a collaborator. It brings all ingredients together to make sense on our taste buds. I'd like to say that salt translates the dish to our receiving tongue. Without it, the meal is tasteless. No matter how good a cook you are, when salt is missing, it tells. That one ingredient can make or break your dish, and appetite.

Jesus said, "You are the salt of the earth..." and He meant it. It's high time you believed it. You are for the taste and for the advantage of others. You're the salt of the earth because you are a binder/ collaborator that helps other people make tasteful sense of living. Through your life and light, others ought to see how life should be lived. That's what Jesus' life is to us; an example that showed us how life ought to be lived as man.

"Our lives are a Christ-like fragrance rising up to God. But this fragrance is perceived differently by those who are being saved and by those who are perishing" (2 Corinthians 2:15 NLT)

We are not only the salt of the earth for taste, we are the fragrance of Christ on earth. As Christians in a living relationship with Jesus, the fragrance of our lives should be a sweet smell rising to GOD. As living sacrifices, constantly on the altar, on fire for Him, we give off a distinct aroma that goes up to please GOD. Be clear about this: your life will always give off a fragrance, no matter what. But whether it's sweet or foul depends on what burns in you. The degree to which you lead your life on this ever-burning altar of life, and how you express or don't express GOD through it. That is what gives off your fragrance. According to 2 Corinthians 2:15, this fragrance is also perceived by the world around us. Just as the smoke and smell of a physical burnt offering on the altar can be perceived by those around it, so can the fragrance of our lives be perceived by those around us. That's part of what people call aura: the fragrance of your life. We can give off different aromas based on what is ablaze in us and whatever we give off can also be interpreted differently based on the receiver. 2 Corinthians 2:16 elaborates: "To those who are perishing, we are a dreadful smell of death and doom. But to those who are being saved, we are a life-giving perfume…" Notice this has nothing to do with the type of fragrance your life produces. It's more about how others interpret your fragrance and what it triggers in them. Your fragrance either convicts them or encourages them. So, it is possible that GOD perceives one thing from your fragrance and some men perceive another thing.

Jesus is always our example. He is the first fruit for so many reasons. In Him, we find value and meaning for life; the very reason for life is in Him. In Him, we live, we breathe, and derive our being. While the salvation and redemption of our souls were of utmost importance to Jesus, our victorious living is equally as important to Him. Ask yourself: if all that was required was the shedding of blood, why did Jesus have to live for so long in the flesh? He could have shed His blood at five years of age or even as an infant, and the blood would have still atoned for our sins. But there is a special significance to why He lived.

Let me remind you that every move GOD makes is for a purpose. Each move is significant to His master plan. Here are my thoughts on why His life was so significant: Jesus lived so that we can see how living was intended to be. Before Jesus, man took his best guess on how life ought to be lived. But Jesus lived so we could get a glimpse of what living looked like when done right. His life was only a glimpse because greater and much more is possible when a man surrenders to GOD. He lived so that we could be stirred up to live the same way. It was through Him we perceived and could truly and completely translate the ingredients of life into victorious living. Without Jesus, many were just whining through life. But with Jesus, we win at living. This is one of the reasons The Holy Spirit is essential to our lives. He is our helper in more ways than can be documented. He is all for aiding us to achieve a victorious life.

The first fruit is set apart from the whole harvest and dedicated unto GOD. The remaining of the harvest are the same as the first fruit — we share the same characteristics. The whole harvest honors GOD. You are the salt of the earth because through you the world can be perceived rightly. Many were lost and didn't know how to lead victorious lives until Jesus. You have the same task. Your experiences and your wins translate the ingredients of your life to the receiving tongue of others. Just as salt is not salty for its own sake, your win is not solely for you. You must fulfill purpose in translating "meals" to the tongues of others.

GET UNDERSTANDING

"In all thy getting, get understanding". Understand why you have adopted these excuses and reverse engineer those beliefs. Identify why these serve as crutches for you. What are you really afraid of? Why have you excused yourself out of displaying your fullness? I'll end this chapter with this quote originally written by Marianne Williamson in her book, A Return to Love: Reflections on the Principle of a Course in Miracles:

> *"Our deepest fear is not that we are inadequate. Our deepest fear is that we are powerful beyond measure. It is our light, not our darkness that most frightens us. We ask ourselves, 'who am I to be brilliant, gorgeous, talented, fabulous'? Who are you not to be? You are a child of God. Your decision to play small does not serve the world. There is nothing enlightened about shrinking so that other people won't feel insecure around you. We are all meant to shine, as children do. We were born to make manifest the glory of God that is within us. It's not just in some of us; it's in everyone. And as we let our own light shine, we unconsciously give other people permission to do the same. As we are liberated from our own fear, our presence automatically liberates others."*

Understand this: You have no excuses, none at all. Not one thing will serve as a reason why you can be excused from winning at life and destiny.

5

REFUSE EVERY LIMITATION

One quiet evening, my attention was suddenly drawn to an outlet on the wall. As I examined it, I found myself trying to imagine a world of outlets: if they could think, what would outlets think of themselves? How would an outlet perceive its existence? Take a good look at an outlet close by and imagine along with me.

I imagined in a world where everyone desires to be whole and complete, its three holes would be considered weaknesses, preventing it from being as wholesome as the wall in which its embedded. And as I pondered on the holes, my attention was drawn to the fact that each hole was intentionally carved into it by its manufacturer. Each hole had a purpose. Without these holes, there would be no access to the electricity it holds. The presence of the holes allows the outlet to be available and used for a greater good. But all of these benefits and good are unknown to Mr. Outlet, as he focuses on his "weaknesses" and thinks to himself "I am not whole".

GOD then whispered to me, saying, "the same goes for those things you call weaknesses in your life. They were carved into the fabric of your existence by design, even by your creator. They are built into your mold for a greater good, if only you could see it that way."

Sometimes, we are so focused on our weaknesses, we miss the benefits they could bring to us and to others. Let's be clear about one thing before we proceed: a weakness is not a weakness until you make it one. Regardless of what you have come to define as imperfect, you must remember GOD does not create imperfections. Everything He created is perfectly fit for the purpose He created it. When you learn to see your so-called weaknesses as intended by design (that is, for a greater good), you'll understand they aren't designed to limit, but elevate you. However, the problem is we've been looking at our "holes" from a perspective other than what was intended by GOD. That needs to change.

> Your "weaknesses" are not designed to limit you. They are designed to elevate you.

PERSPECTIVE MATTERS

"There is no such thing as impossible; the word itself says "I'm possible"" - *Audrey Hepburn*

How you see what you see matters a lot. The first time I read that quote by Audrey Hepburn, I was blown away. And I haven't been able to shake it off since then. Its core message: perspective matters! For the first time in my life, I had come face to face with the power of perspective. The same word, viewed differently, transformed the idea of impossibility to possibility. The same word intended to defeat, turned into what fuels courage, simply by rearranging how you see what you see. The lesson? A simple reorganization of your viewpoint about any situation can make a mountain of difference.

By definition, I am what is known as an introvert. In this particular instance, I refer to the 'shy and reserved' definition. There was a point in time, however, when I hated that label, and even thought of it as a handicap. Well, when I think about it now, I probably hated the label because of the way others viewed introverts. When I was younger, people made being quiet and reserved a bad thing. Some people thought I was just stuck up, and for a long time, I didn't even know how to refute it. I wasn't stuck up. I was just an introvert. If only they knew I wanted to play with them… I just couldn't help but observe first. And since most people hold first impressions as the truth, many concluded that I wasn't friendly or, worse still, was full of myself. This was far from the truth. I was just the type to study my environment before participating. I enjoyed time with myself more comfortably than time spent in a crowd. Being reserved in new environments did not mean I wouldn't go exploring, it just meant I would first sit and map out how I wanted to go about it, who I wanted to talk to first, where I wanted to start my exploring, and so on. The world didn't understand that, and at first, neither did I. My environment, therefore, taught me to dislike my introverted nature. I was advised by many to change my nature; I needed to mingle more, make more friends, speak up more, do this more and do that more. It just made me feel like who I was and how I expressed myself was not enough. The world wanted more; more than I had and all I had to give was me.

It took GOD to undo that damage – that warped idea that I wasn't good enough, that I needed to change. I wanted Him to change me and I demanded it of Him many days. I didn't want to be an introvert anymore. However, no matter how many times I cried out to Him, GOD refused to change me. He didn't want me to change; He created me that way for a purpose. I didn't like His decision at first because I felt a change would've taken away all the angst I had in my world. But I have learnt when GOD is silent, it's for our own good. He doesn't give us the answer we desire because it would cost us more. But we cry, and cry some more, because we can't see the whole picture. We're oblivious to all that's ahead and how our personality fits into His plan. In my case, GOD's 'silence' was loud and clear. He responded to my prayers but just not with what I was hoping for.

It's almost always easier to tear down; building up requires much more effort. You can demolish a house in a few hours, maybe even minutes, but days are required to build one. Well, maybe except for that one time when the amazing Habitat for Humanity organization built a house in less than 4 hours. To be precise, some 200 volunteers of the Habitat for Humanity in Shelby County, Alabama built a three-bedroom, two-bath house in 3 hours, 26 minutes and 34 seconds! That's pretty amazing, huh?

But it usually doesn't work that way; this example was an exception when building a house. It certainly didn't work that way in rebuilding me. It took a while to build up what my perceived limitations had torn down in my world. Once one adopts limitations, these perceived limitations can easily tear down one's confidence, and the effort required in building oneself back up again isn't as easy. But what if we decided to not only build ourselves back up, but also tear down the ideas that have limited us for so long. Let's focus on tearing down the limitations. After all, it is easier to tear down, right?

GIVE ME YOUR EYES

If we could see ourselves through GOD's eyes, it would transform how we see ourselves and eventually transform who we are. GOD sees us differently. He sees our so-called weaknesses differently. If we believe in GOD, we must, therefore, adopt a different perspective on life and begin to see our weaknesses differently. Just like those ten letters — IMPOSSIBLE — we can view them differently and see them as: I'M POSSIBLE. Know this with confidence: if GOD put those weaknesses there, there is good in them.

My grace is sufficient for you; because My power is being perfected [and is completed and shows itself most effectively] in [your] weakness." Therefore, I will all the more gladly boast in my weaknesses, so that the power of Christ [may completely enfold me and] may dwell in me. (2 Corinthians 12:9 AMP)

And there goes their good! Those so-called weaknesses are portals through which GOD pours His power into our lives. Rather than focus on them as weaknesses, and allowing them to transform into limitations, focus on GOD and His intent for them. If you focus on the weaknesses, like the outlet focused on his holes, you will stumble on them. But if we focus on GOD and His intended use for them, we'll soar through the very same holes. Allow GOD to plug into those babies. Our weaknesses create an atmosphere for total abandon, in which we must rely and lean totally on GOD to make something out of them. You are required to trust GOD's design, trusting Him even with the very thing you see as a handicap and would naturally want to trade-in. Trust that if He made it part of you, He'll reveal Himself in them. Remember, when we don't know the use of a thing, misuse is inevitable. So be careful, don't misuse your weaknesses!

It's amazing to see that GOD perfects His power through that which makes you feel flawed and insufficient. You can hardly call them weaknesses when you begin to see them with this new perspective. A realization that GOD bonds even more with you, through these so-called weaknesses, alters their very meaning. You can begin to look at them as super strengths more than anything else. To think anyone would look fondly on their weaknesses may be a bit strange. But Paul did it, and now I get why he did! I now see what he saw that moved him to say, "I am glad to boast about my weaknesses". These so-called weaknesses are really in fact the best kept secret portals of strength.

Being an introvert is indeed where my magic happens! It's one of my biggest assets. That reserved and observant nature afforded me insights to things others would easily miss. It contributes to why I can listen long and attentively in my interactions with people. Loving my own company means I rarely feel lonely, and can work independently without anyone looking over my shoulders. I say all this to show that there is strength and beauty in who you are, no matter how the world labels it. As a matter of fact, one of the common themes in the feedback I get from past colleagues is them not needing to hound me to get my tasks done. This, and many more traits, I have found unique to my type of introversion. Once I could view it differently, I saw the power in it.

> Those so-called weaknesses are portals through which GOD pours His power into our lives

So, what changed? Nothing really. Nothing except my perspective. That's all that changed! I didn't stop observing, I didn't need to mingle more, and I still have only a handful of friends. And life has never been better. The best part was I didn't have to do more of anything. Just being me is enough!

BRAVE THE ALTERNATIVE PATH

Excuses are birthed out of small mindedness. When these excuses mix with our perceived weaknesses, we create limitations for ourselves. And when limitations have their way, mediocrity moves in. If we knew better, we wouldn't condone excuses, as they fuel a mediocre mindset. But alas, we make excuses because we have become comfortable with mediocrity — that feeling which makes you settle for the path of least resistance; the one that makes you play safe.

The Path of Least Resistance is defined as a physical or metaphysical pathway that produces the least obstruction to forward movement among other alternative paths. In other words, of all the available paths, it is the easiest and most convenient, the one that doesn't require much from you. The world does a great job convincing us to take the path of least resistance. But this path is another name for that easily beguiling comfort zone. I am convinced anyone that has ever done anything significant, first found themselves in the place where the status quo (comfort zone) was no longer enough. To make something significant of your life, you must not settle for the path of least resistance. To be extraordinary, you must be willing to defy the odds. You must deny the path of least resistance to manifest God's glory in your life. Generations past, present, and future study the plane in flight, not because it took the path of least resistance, but because it defied the odds to brave an alternative path. You will leave a mark in the world when you defy odds.

I once overheard my brother talking to my son about this same principle. As he encouraged my son to excel in his studies, what he said amplified my understanding of the dangers of taking the path of least resistance. My son sat attentively before his uncle, as he tutored him. In admonishing him, my brother said to him, "you see, you don't have to do anything to fail, but you must put in effort to succeed." It was more than mere words to me — it spoke to my core and clarified the ever-present dangers of taking the path of the comfort zone. I also believe my son understood the treasure found in that statement because, to date, I can still hear him use those same words to encourage himself on weary days.

CONSENT MATTERS

Some years ago, I was listening to a sermon about taking one's life by the horns. It must have been something the preacher said, but before I knew it, I was engrossed in a private teaching with The Lord. The Holy Spirit took over and began to lead me into something unrelated to the sermon. Has that ever happened to you? One minute you are listening to someone and, suddenly, their voice becomes a soothing backdrop for a Holy Spirit one-on-one session?

As I sat there, almost in a trance, I realized I had given consent to some things to limit me. Somehow, I had lost my fire to fight, and I was just taking the lemons life gave me, instead of going after what GOD had for me. By the time the teaching was over, I decided to rip up every subconscious agreement to be limited by anything. That day I decided, no more limitations! It doesn't matter how long you've given consent to that idea. Whenever you realize the idea no longer serves you, go ahead and change it. Decide to change course. There is no wisdom in laying in a bed of thorns, just because you made it. It's foolishness to jump into it. And you'll only have yourself to blame, if you do so.

Let me paraphrase Proverbs 27:12: A wise man sees a ditch ahead and changes his course, but the fool sees the same ditch, continues on the path, falls headlong into it, and suffers the consequences. Remember, your senses are designed to inform your decisions. Use them. If you can see the impending danger, GOD is telling you, through your eyes, that you need to change your course. You don't need a thunderous, earth-shaking voice to tell you that. GOD will not do for you what you can do for yourself. He doesn't want you to be lazy!

"But when you decide to break free, you will shake his yoke from your neck," reads Genesis 27:40. I love this scripture with all my heart. I'll give you a quick overview of what led to this. Esau and Jacob were twin brothers born to Isaac and Rebecca. Esau was the older twin and the first-born son to his parents. According to the Jewish Encyclopedia, Jewish customs state that the first born is entitled to a double share of the real and personal estate of the father when he dies. In this case, Isaac understood the real blessing was not in material things, like his properties, but in the prayers he transferred from his spirit to his sons. So, when he sensed that he would die soon, he called his eldest son Esau and asked Esau to prepare him his favorite dish made of game meat. He was to prepare it just the way his father liked it, so that he [Isaac] could eat and confer the blessing from his soul (see Genesis 27:1-46). But while Esau went hunting, Rebecca prepared Jacob to receive the prayers in his brother's place. With a dish in hand and a great disguise, so that his arms felt hairy like Esau's, Jacob went before his father. Isaac, whose eyes were dim, couldn't tell the difference and blessed Jacob with what he intended for Esau. When Esau came back, and found out what happened, he cried to his father to reverse the irreversible. Although Isaac couldn't undo his prayers for Jacob, he gave Esau a key that I'm sure he didn't realize at the time.

The key was simple: when you decide to break free, you will. All Esau had to do, to break free of the yoke and burden placed on him by this mishap, was to decide. It seemed way too simple. Maybe if it were something more complicated, he would have caught it that very day. To be honest, I would have missed it too. And this right here is a problem many people have in today's world. The simplicity in Christ is why most (people) push Him and His instructions away. They think to themselves: "that's it?!" It seems too simple to make a difference. But the best things in life are not just free; GOD has also made them simple.

Yokes have only one purpose: to restrict. They are limitations. Esau's dreadful experience could have been a perennial limitation. Among other things, the devil could have capitalized on that situation, to break and turn him away from his purpose, and ultimately from GOD. But thank GOD for the key. I don't know if Esau recognized it as a key when his father said those words. Maybe he just suddenly realized that choosing the past over the present kills the future. One way or the other, Esau decided. He decided he no longer wanted to be bound by the past, and by all that was done or not done. He changed his mind toward the whole situation and life began anew for him. The proof is in his reunion with his brother. By the time he saw his brother again, he had greatly multiplied with family, servants, and wealth of his own. He was able to welcome his brother with joy and love. That kind of change couldn't have happened without Esau making a conscious decision. By deciding to shake off the yoke, he shook off many years of limitations and small mindedness.

THE LIMITATION THAT ONCE HELD ME

As a foreign student in the United States, the cost of a college education was made worst by the fact that I didn't have access to financial aid. I worked, but wasn't earning enough to pay my way through college. So, after some years of struggling with finances, and not being eligible for federal grants and loans, I was forced to quit college till I could afford to finish. At first everything was fine. I boldly went on job interviews, and nabbed any job I set my sights on. It was great because the degree, or the lack of one, didn't really stop anything. The one thing that GOD helped me to do was to continue acquiring knowledge even though I wasn't going into a classroom to learn. I self-learned many subjects of interest and

I loved the flexibility of learning exactly what I wanted. By the grace of GOD, you wouldn't have been able to tell that I didn't have a college degree. Then, I set my eyes on a position at a global pharmaceutical company. Everything seemed okay at first. As a matter of fact, I was seven months pregnant with our first child when I went on the interview and I was offered the position. I was to start the job after I gave birth and it was all going to work out. But then one cold morning, I got a call from the company's HR representative that the offer was being rescinded. "Why?" I asked, stunned. She said: "We are sorry, but you do not have a bachelor's degree. It is an absolute requirement for this position." I was speechless. I didn't know what to say or do. It hadn't been an issue till then. And right there, the certificate that had never stopped me before, stopped me dead in my tracks.

The lack of a degree had officially become a limitation. I couldn't get past it and I automatically thought no one would hire me because I didn't have it. Ignorantly, it didn't matter that in earlier years, it hadn't stopped me. Suddenly, it became a wall I couldn't go through, and my testimony was going to change. I resulted to playing safe and taking jobs that were grades below my experience and qualifications, simply because I didn't have a piece of paper to prove I had the understanding. If the job required a degree, or even equivalent experience as some would note, I didn't even bother. I shied away from it. That same note was on the job that seemingly brought me to my knees when I had applied for it.

But as I sat in my Holy Spirit initiated session on that Sunday morning, it was clear: I had given consent to playing small because of one bad try. That day, I realized education and a paper that certifies you are educated are two different things. My proof was in me, not in the certificate. I got wind beneath my wings in that session; the permission to soar with or without a piece of paper! It was going to require work on my part, but I was ready to give it my all. I had to sell myself more at each interview, knowing they required proof. Since I didn't have the kind they were used to, I made up my mind to leave every meeting having amazed my interviewers. And so, I did. I went out on a limb one more time and GOD did it.

The following month, I was back to school. GOD had put a new fire in me, and I could not be stopped. Every lie that used to hold me back had been burnt up, consumed by the fire of the conviction that burned through me during my Holy Spirit private session. All the knowledge I had acquired over the years gave me great insights and an edge in my classes. I completed college with no stress, as the knowledge was already within me. Within a year, I was graduating, and my own degree wasn't proof of being knowledgeable. It was proof that when you decide to break free, you too will shake the yoke off your shoulders. More importantly, I was offered a job within that same month of going back to school. The best part being I still didn't have a degree at the time I was offered the dream job. In fact, nothing had changed outwardly; but within me, everything had changed. I gave myself permission to be. You see, when you decide, you will change your world.

Revisit those agreements. Reaffirm the healthy ones and rip the negative contracts. Agree no more with the things that don't agree with your win.

It's only a limitation for as long
as you consent to it being one.

WHAT'S AT STAKE

Think about it for a second: what's the effect of embracing limitations and adopting a mediocre mindset? I'll give you one more second to think about it.

I thought about the times in my life in which I played small, and one thing was glaring...I felt miserable! It started out as frustration, and soon grew into misery, because I knew I was made for more — I just knew I could do much better! The fact that I wasn't doing better bothered me very much. When you know there's so much inside of you, but you can't seem to get it out; or you unconsciously suppress it because of a limitation you have set in place, you are bound to be frustrated. There are times you may not even know why you feel so miserable. It feels like a tug of war within you when you unconsciously limit yourself; yet you feel restricted and caged in because you truly desire to birth what's within. The same person that wants to burst forth is the same person that has unconsciously placed a limit on how far they can go. Isn't that a serious conflict of interest?

Limitations are like an invisible barrier that prevents a basketball player's shot from going into the basket. The barrier places a limit on how far the ball can go, no matter how hard the player tries. It wouldn't matter how tall the player is or just how skilled he is; the barrier will prevent him from making the shot. As a matter of fact, the harder he throws the ball, the swifter the ball bounces back at him. No matter how hard he tries, he won't accomplish much without first eliminating the barrier.

Many times, we are oblivious to the things that limit us. They seem invisible to us, and that makes for a very frustrating experience. Hindsight is always 20/20, and I can tell you that during the years I took a backseat, because I didn't have a degree, I wasn't aware I was limiting myself. I didn't know I had adopted a mediocre mindset until that Holy Spirit intervention. I just thought I was doing the best with what I had. Many people believe when life gives you a lemon, you just ought to make lemonade. But let me do you one better. When life gives you lemons, trade it in for what you really want. Don't just make do with what you have. Making lemonade is making do with what you have. Trade it up. Go bargaining with it. Life is all about trade-offs. I had to do a trade-off to secure those jobs. I traded with what I had, to get what I needed. I brought my experience and knowledge to the table. Trading always changes whatever is in your hands and the beauty of it is you will never end up with what you started with. You might start with lemons and end up with honey, or, in my case, start with knowledge and experience without a degree, and end up with a job that would normally require one.

Limitations make us miserable! They rob us of fulfillment and satisfaction in our lives. They alter the feel of our existence: how we feel about our own life and the impact our lives have on others. Think of your life as a budding flower. Limitations cause the flower to stay closed, even when the sun is out. And that, my friends, has a profound effect. One, it cuts off the flower from fully benefiting from the sun — its source of light and energy, and essential for its growth. Sooner or later, if the chlorophyll on the plant does not receive light, the plant will die and the flower is prevented from experiencing its own fullness. And secondly, it robs the world of the beauty they would have beheld if the flower had blossomed. How does that relate to us? Here's how: limitations prevent us from getting a full picture of what GOD would have us do or be. And it prevents us from receiving the power essential for our living and the fulfillment of our purpose. GOD is the sun of our lives, the source of our light. He is the one that lights up every man that comes into the world (see John1:1-5). He sustains and energizes us by the power of His light in this dark world.

Limitations stop us where we are, and makes it difficult to experience more than we already know. We will never know how life could be, until we move the limitations out of the way. They must not hinder you from manifesting the fullness GOD intends for your life. Limitations in a man's life cheats the world of the beauty he ought to experience as part of the fullness of his manifestation.

The glow of our light (as lights of the earth) ought to spread abroad and reach into the lives of others. The radiance of the light awakens others who may be asleep. It gives clarity to others who are lost, brings peace to those who have been surrounded by shadows, and rips the covers off darkness so others may find their own light. All these are at stake when we embrace limitations. The entire world suffers when we don't reach your highest potential.

6

REFUSE SIN

Sin is probably one of the most unpopular subjects in the world. Many people don't want to talk about it, and even more people don't want to hear about it. But it is slowly taking over the nooks and crannies of our society. For a thing costing us so much, I'm really not sure why people are so averse to dealing with it. For many, it's a case of "speak no evil, hear no evil". Some who are unwilling to talk about it are wary about making others uncomfortable, due to the guilt that tends to come with identifying one's wrong doings. Others don't want to talk about it because it would mean coming to terms with their own sins. Those who don't want to hear about it are reluctant they don't want the piercing of the conscience that comes with hearing about their sins, especially when they feel helpless against its grip on their lives. All of these parties would rather ignore the pink elephant in the room. Regardless of how we feel, however, about talking or hearing about sin, the truth is everyone knows it exists and we can no longer afford to shy away from it. Hosea 4:6 says "*My people are destroyed for lack of knowledge*", and I believe ignorance on the issue of sin is what is fueling its power against us as a people. So, let's shed some light on this topic and I strongly pray that the Lord will help you see what sin is and His laid out plan against it.

WHAT'S AT STAKE?

Let's start with what's at stake, if we keep on living in sin. Sin can seem attractive; it can seem good, pleasant and desirable; but its consequences are dire. In the beginning, in the garden of Eden, GOD said to man, "*you must not eat from the tree of the knowledge of good and evil [the tree of death]; for when you eat from it, you will certainly die*". The consequences of sin have not changed since then. Sin always results in death. But just as Adam was deceived when he first bit into that forbidden fruit, even so, men are still deceived today. Many don't understand what GOD means by, "you will certainly die", especially because they don't literally cease to exist when they partake of sin. But just because we do not drop dead at the instance of sin doesn't mean a death has not occurred. By now, it should be clear that every word GOD speaks is like a thousand words spoken. When Adam partook of the first sin, he didn't drop dead, but he did shift from one form of existence into another. Man officially shifted from operating from spirit to operating from the natural, signifying the death of the original order; the intended form of existence. A death occurs every time we engage in sinful acts, 'killing' our spirit with every single corrupt action. The more we engage in sinful acts, the more we corrupt our spirit. And as a virus corrupts a computer system, and it begins to malfunction, even so sin corrupts a man and he also malfunctions.

THE WEIGHT OF SIN

I used to think sin was simply the items on the "thou shall not" list. You know the list; the ten commandments. And I was certain that if I complied with that list, then I would have victory over sin. That was until I came across this verse: *"You have heard that it was said to those of old, 'You shall not commit adultery.' But I say to you that whoever looks at a woman to lust for her has already committed adultery with her in his heart..." (Matthew 5:27)*

My interpretation of that verse: sin is more than a list, and it's of a much wider spectrum than the ten commandments can convey. I thought adultery occurred only when a married person goes outside of their marriage to have sexual relations with someone else. But here was Jesus, showing us a different dimension of just one of the ten commandments, in such a way that had never been seen or thought of before. In this single verse, Jesus expanded our understanding of the word adultery. And I suddenly get this gut feeling that each one of the other commandments could be expatiated in a thousand different ways. Every single word GOD speaks can be both literal and figurative and so, with GOD, one word is like a thousand words and a thousand words are like one word. This proves that there may be much more substance to what we know (or think we know). In that moment, I realized sin was more than I knew it to be. So, I sought GOD for more understanding.

Sin is not a list of do-nots.

A few days later, awakening from a night's rest, it came to me! GOD dropped a clear definition for sin in my knower. Sin is misuse! Sin is the misuse of anything GOD created; it's the wrong use of a good thing. You can misuse anything: your eyes, your mouth, your thoughts, your time, your moments, your body, your gifts, your intellect, your influence, your power, your child, your spouse, your friend, animate and inanimate objects, even tangible and intangible things alike. Misuse connotes an improper application or use of a thing. Sin, therefore, is malfunction at play.

The question now is: misuse according to who? It's important to straighten this out because more and more people are getting confused about what GOD frowns or doesn't frown upon. The reason is because, in various societies, many have muddied the waters of what GOD says He dislikes. I have had many conversations in which people ask me if something is a sin or not. And I have asked the same question of others when things were not clear. But like anything that exists in our world, if no one else knows how to use it, at the very least, the product's manufacturer knows exactly how it ought to function and what would constitute a misuse. So, here's the simple answer to that question: "misuse according to GOD". Only GOD truly knows the right use of anything and everything, animate or inanimate, tangible or intangible in every given moment.

Another way to look at sin is disobedience. When we misuse anything GOD created, we have simply disobeyed GOD's intention for that thing.

Sin is misuse.
Sin is disobedience.

WHO HAS ASKED THIS OF YOU?

If you're anything like me, your next thoughts after that revelation are: How could I now win against this enemy known as sin? How do I stay away from sin? These thought came to me and they almost seemed to cripple me before I could even think of possible solutions. Pressed under the weight of this new truth, I heard GOD ask me "who has asked this of you?" My response: 'Wait, what?'

Then, suddenly, the understanding came rushing in like a flood. Yes, GOD requires a sinless life of us, but He hasn't asked that we do it on our own. As a matter of fact, He hasn't asked anything of our own will & power. Whenever there is heavy lifting to be done, be rest assured, it will always fall on GOD to do the heavy lifting. He doesn't want us taking on responsibilities that are not ours. He asked, "who has asked this of you?" because He knew I thought it was in *my* power to stay above sin. But I wasn't required to do any more about sin than had already been done.

You have been deceived! We all have! This whole time we thought GOD wanted us to do something about this thing we are so helpless against. We thought He required us to do it all by ourselves. Whereas, all He wants is to be all of it for us: our righteousness, our holiness, our sinlessness,...our perfection! And until we end the use of self-will and self-power, we won't accept the all-enabling, all-supporting power of the The Almighty. He wants to work us into perfect harmonies, not by our own doing, but by His. GOD already did all the heavy lifting in the humbling sacrifice of Jesus. It is not required of you, in your own strength and power, to crush sin; sin has already been crushed for you. The problem is most of us still act like we are under sin's grip, and consequently make choices supporting that myth. It's the case of the fly in a closed jar. While the lid is on, the fly can only fly so high, the lid restricting its altitude. But surprisingly, even when the lid is removed, you will observe the fly still maintaining the familiar boundaries. This is because the fly has been restricted by the lid for so long that it has gotten used to the restriction. Same thing applies to us here. We are so accustomed to the weight of sin that, even now that it has been revoked, we ignorantly act like those still bound by it. We are no longer bound by sin! The lid of sin, that old constrain, has been lifted, and we are free from its shackles forever. Whoever the Lord sets free is free indeed; and He declares you free!

YOU CAN WIN OVER SIN

First, believe! You can't achieve what you don't believe. Overtime we have bought into the notion that it's impossible to live life sinless. And so, we are find ourselves defeated before we can even start. Believe in GOD's design and His provision for you. Believe that He won't require out of your hands what He hasn't already put within your reach. Believe that if GOD says you are free from sin, then you truly are. One thing that always encourages me is the model Man: Jesus. If He, as a man, lived above sin, so can I by the same power that was at work in Him.

Once you believe, surrender! Surrender to every desire of GOD. As He leads, you must follow in surrender. Many times, we ask GOD to strengthen us against sin, but we really ought to ask that He helps us to surrender more completely to Him in all that we do. When a soldier surrenders at war to his opponent, he is saying, 'I will become his servant and will now begin to follow his commands only'. In that surrender, he makes himself subject to the instructions, customs, and will of his opponent. We cannot live above sin by strength but by surrender.

Whosoever is born of God does not commit sin; for His seed remains in him; and he cannot sin, because he is born of God. 1 John 3:9

At first this verse was a big challenge to me because I just couldn't understand it. I had given my life to Christ — confessed Him as my Lord and savior — and had asked Him to take over my life; but I could still find sin present within me. I didn't want to do certain things, but I couldn't help myself. My life became living proof of the struggle Paul spoke about in Roman 1:15 when he said, "I don't really understand myself, for I want to do what is right, but I don't do it. Instead I do what I hate". I couldn't understand why old things didn't quite pass away when I gave my life to Christ; why all things were not made new. Some things were new but not all things were new. Although I had given my life to Christ, I was still lying. That was my struggle. Lies. And since the scripture is both literal and figurative, every time I read that verse literally, my heart would sink. It sunk because the idea that I must not be of GOD, if sin was still present in me, challenged me. I longed for the day when all things would indeed become new. For many years, I pacified myself with other more tolerable translations of that verse that suggested a milder meaning. One in particular suggested it meant that I wouldn't desire to sin. That was comfortable, after all I didn't desire to sin. And whenever I did sin, I didn't want to continue in it anyway.

But regardless of my false comfort, this verse was ingrained in my head. My heart would often mull over it, and I would continuously resolve to pacifying myself again and again. Then one day, I was on my way to pick up the boys from school when GOD came knocking. It started with a question. He asked, "What does it mean to be born of GOD." The answer came as quickly as the question: "to be born of GOD means you are a child of GOD". He went further and asked, "but who are the real children of GOD?" The first thought was, 'Jesus is the son of GOD, He is a real child of GOD'. Then suddenly, I remembered an account of Jesus in the synagogue, when someone came to Him saying, "your mother and brothers are looking for you". To that person, Jesus answered and said, "*Who is My mother and who are My brothers?*" And then He stretched out His hand toward His disciples and said, "*Here are My mother and My brothers! For whoever does the will of My Father in heaven is My brother and sister and mother.*" (Read Matthew 12:46-50) And the understanding rushed in all at once! If being born of GOD means you are a child of GOD, and obedience to GOD is the only thing that proves you as a child of GOD, whosoever is in total surrender and obedience to GOD, cannot sin. He can not sin because sin is misuse, and GOD will not instruct you in misuse. He can't sin because sin is disobedience and he who is in constant obedience can not sin.

This blew my mind! The very solution to this very old culprit of wholeness is in simple obedience.

This now amplifies the importance of our choices. In surrender, you must choose only that which GOD chooses. Your choices are how you cast your ballot in surrender. When you choose what GOD chooses, you are in total surrender. Otherwise, you really haven't surrendered. Confessing Jesus as Lord and Savior is only an introduction to the life we ought to live. Having given our lives to Him, we must now begin to align our choices with His, so we can truly live out the desired sinless life He purposed for us. But what happens when He leads and we don't follow? Well then, we are no different from how our lives were before we confessed

Him as Lord. When true change happens, your choices will reflect the change that has happened.

MORE INNATE

At this point, let me address one of the concepts that crippled me for a very long time. This concept attempts to reduce, in our minds, the completed work of Christ on the issue of sin. For many years, I couldn't get past the concept of having a "sin nature". If my original nature can not but sin, it sounds like I was create to sin. But that is not true!

Sin is not your *original* nature! It was introduced along the line. The bible says, "*[a] good tree bears good fruit, [and] a bad tree bears bad fruit. A good tree cannot bear bad fruit, and a bad tree cannot bear good fruit*". You are a good tree born out of The Good Tree — GOD. GOD cannot bare bad fruits because He is good! Good is more innate to you than evil. Before the serpent beguiled Eve, man was perfect in GOD. The original model, the original make up of man was of GOD. Sin was an infection to the perfect mold. To believe this infection has negated the good material with which you were created in the first place, is to not understand the very material you were made of. I had to renew my mind in this truth to rouse up my GOD dormant genes. GOD's genes (His seed) lives within us and when we allow that seed to become active rather than dormant within us, we cannot sin!

Sin might be our natural state, but it's not our original state. That first disobedience (the eating of the forbidden fruit) tuned man to live from his natural self rather than from his original — spirit — self. From the day man bit into that fruit, the natural man gained dominance over the spirit man. Nonetheless, man is first a spiritual being before he is natural, and when he no longer operates in this natural form, he'll revert to his spiritual state. For this cause, Christ came and died: to crucify the natural man and take him out of the way so that the spiritual man can triumph even in this realm; to revert the disorder that was introduced by that great disobedience. His death as a natural man brought an awakening of the spirit of every man, that same spirit that was once dormant within us, so that we can live triumphant lives through that same spirit.

Sin is not your original state.

7

THE BIG SECRET

There is a secret to winning — one that is guaranteed. I can assure you that if you understand this secret, and apply its principles, you will always win. It's very simple, yet it is this simplicity that makes many doubt it. I think it ties back to the idea that life is complicated, and so the solutions to challenges we face ought to be just as complicated. We understand simple solutions for simple problems, but we usually cannot fathom the concept of simple solutions for difficult problems. But GOD's ways are simply not our ways. His ways are light years better than ours and in the same manner, they are much simpler than the solutions we cook up.

We must learn to take GOD simply at His word and really believe that He means whatsoever He says. The simplicity of His word is where our breakthrough lies. We must learn to take His word at face value. Don't read more into it than is necessary. Some people are so good at reading between the lines, they read between lines, even when there are none. Others think GOD always speaks in parables. He does speak in parables, but He speaks plainly as well. GOD has made things simple and plain to eliminate confusion. But what needless pain we bear when we refuse the simplicity that is in Him.

I can understand man's thought pattern. The natural man is rational; he operates within logic. So, it makes logical sense for simple solutions to work out simple issues and difficult solutions to work out difficult issues. But we must never forget that the foolishness of GOD is greater than the wisdom of men, and that His weakness is stronger than our greatest strength. His ways are indeed, 'as far as the heavens are from the earth', far away from our ways. GOD chooses to strengthen weaknesses and ridicule strengths: 1) to highlight His sovereignty and His awesome might; there's simply nothing He cannot do, and 2) to remind man that he is just man, and without Him, GOD, man cannot do much. He has chosen the simple things and has exalted them, even the 'foolish' things, above all others. You must embrace them too, as therein lies the answers to the most difficult of situations. Enough of choosing to grope in the dark, just because we fail to accept the simple ways GOD prescribes. He simplified it all with us in mind. When we cherish what GOD cherishes, love what GOD loves and value what GOD values, life becomes truly simple.

SIMPLE IS NOT EASY

We cannot fathom simple solutions mostly because we misconstrue the word simple to also mean easy. But that is not always the case. As a matter of fact, I have found it mostly untrue. The simple things are not always the easiest of things to do. An example is believing GOD. As simple as it sounds, many people don't believe GOD because believing GOD requires more than just believing God. Sometimes, it requires looking like a fool and loving it. Other times, it requires refusing what you see with your natural eyes, refusing what you hear with your natural ears, and refusing everything you think you know. Believing means simply relying on GOD. As simple as that sounds, it is quite difficult to actualize.

There are situations in which everything within you is in driving you in one direction, but the word of GOD says you must go the other. It's simple enough to know that God's way is the best, but choosing His way isn't that easy. When your brain and everything is saying don't be a fool, you must choose to be one.

•••••••

Some years ago, I got a crash course on loving to be a fool. I was on my way to work, with one of my colleagues, when she mentioned that she had a headache. My first thought was to pray, but I remember being hesitant. I was hesitant because I thought, 'what if I prayed and nothing happened?'. Almost immediately, I could hear GOD whisper to me "you must be willing to look foolish". I suddenly realized the only reason I didn't want to pray for her was because I didn't want to look like the fool who went out on a limb praying for her Hindu friend and nothing happened. I was concerned about how it would look on me and forgot the fact I wasn't on the line. When we pray, it's never about us. It's about The One to whom we pray. When our focus is on us, it becomes all about us. And whether we realize it or not, in that moment, we intend the glory for ourselves. In turn, we lose out on the chance to be a channel through which heaven's reality permeates earth's.

Miracles happen at the corner of foolish and faith

With my friend, I didn't want to be a fool. But we have not been called to work by sight or logic. So, I summoned courage and asked if I could pray with her. She said yes and I prayed. I honestly don't know if anything happened about her headache because I was still apprehensive about the whole thing and didn't ask to confirm. But honestly, all I wanted was to be fool enough to pray in that moment. While I can't testify she was healed that day, I know I was. Something shifted in me. You must dare to be a fool in the face of impossibilities. The natural reaction, when facing what man would call impossible, is to quit or go home. But real winners are those who stand in the face of such impossibilities and stare it down in faith, till it backs down. That day, I realized miracles mostly happen at the corner of foolish and faith. Praying is simple enough but it wasn't easy for me that day.

•••••••

Let's examine one more situation. GOD's plan required His son, Jesus, to die for all men, paying the price once and for all, so that all may live. Seems simple enough, right? But how easy do you think it was for Christ to accomplish that? It doesn't matter what He was in that moment, GOD-Man, Man or GOD. The truth is the flesh still pains when whipped, the heart still breaks when wrongly accused, and thoughts to save oneself first still came to Him. He just refused them; He chose to be mute through it all. Think about the suffering He endured to accomplish that simple plan. You can, at least, relate to the temptations of sin that came His way. I'm sure you can relate because you know just how difficult it is to shun sin in your own life. Think of the shame and humiliation He went through at the hands of men — His own creation. Think of the cross where He displayed such determination to follow through on the plan. He could have vindicated Himself and left us to our impending doom. Do you realize if Jesus had saved Himself from the cross, He wouldn't stop being GOD? It wouldn't make Him any less who He is, and guess what? No one can hold Him accountable for not going through with it. He makes and tweaks rules at His whim; all for His glory. We wouldn't even know enough to accuse Him. But Jesus chose to be a fool for our sakes. Hallelujah!

THE ONE BIG THING

After studying great men and women of GOD across the world, I observed a common trait. This same trait is visible in the great men and women of the Bible. This one trait makes ordinary men super humans. It's also the same thing that stands out perfectly in all that Jesus said and did

"If Jesus did all He did as GOD, I am impressed but I am not compelled to follow. But, if Jesus did all He did as a man, then I am compelled to follow suit," opines Pastor Bill Johnson. Let me start by saying this statement above does not reduce the deity of Christ as some claim. The truth is we couldn't reduce it, even if we tried. Rather, it's a statement that simply focuses on his humanity. I have come to realize the humanity and deity of Christ existed in a oneness beyond human comprehension. Our best attempt to understand it would only be scratching the surface. We can try, but we will fall short. Way short of the reality GOD made present in Christ. More importantly, what I gather from this statement is, if you dare to follow in Christ's footsteps, you will go down the same paths and have similar experiences as He had. Imagine a little child stepping into the footsteps of his father. While he may not see all that his father saw, owing to differences in height, personality, and preferences, the little child would experience life in his own unique way through his father's path. That's what I believe Bill Johnson alludes to. Therefore, if we must follow in the footsteps of Christ, we must find His footsteps and fit right into them. But if we must do that, we must examine something Christ told us about Himself. This, I believe, is the secret to our win.

GOD might talk a lot but He is no talkative. He doesn't just talk because He loves to hear His own voice. Every word has a purpose and every repetition is supposed to drill the word deeper into us. In the Psalms, David recalls: *".... once has GOD spoken, twice have I heard it."* So, when GOD speaks five times, how many times must we hear? At least 10, right? In the book of John, Jesus explains: "I tell you the truth, the Son can do nothing by himself. He does only what he sees the Father doing. Whatever the Father does, the Son also does (John 5:19 [variations of the same thing can be found in John 5:30, 8:28, 12:49, 14:10-11. And I intentionally chose only one of the gospels to eliminate duplicates]). As mentioned earlier, we must take GOD at His word, especially His testimony about Himself. No one can tell you about Jesus better than Jesus. He is telling us plainly and simply He only does what GOD, The Father, says to do and says to say. Without The Father, The Son can do nothing!

Still wondering what the common trait is? OBEDIENCE! It's the one big thing that makes all the difference.

The man, Jesus, functioned in the fullness of His purpose, and lived out a fulfilling life, simply because He was obedient to GOD. Of His obedience, it is written: *"He humbled himself in obedience to God and [even obedience unto death] on a cross. Therefore, God elevated him to the place of highest honor and gave him the name above all other names, that at the name of Jesus every knee should bow, in heaven and on earth and under the earth, and every tongue declare that Jesus Christ is Lord, to the glory of God, the Father".*

Let's take a look at the fruits of Jesus' obedience: 1) GOD

elevated and honored Him, 2) GOD gave Him a name above all others, 3) GOD made it so everything created would be subject to Him, restoring the original plan of giving dominion over all that was created to a man, and 4) GOD made all things recognize Him as Lord, whether they liked it or not. Isn't that a winning life? Jesus lived that life here on earth, and now even more in the fullness of His glory, as He sits at the right hand of GOD, The Father, ruling and judging all. He won simply because He obeyed! You can too. The key is simple. Let me be frank: without GOD, you can do nothing! All that is accomplished outside of Him is corruptible and will surely fade away. Stick to him. Obey him. Your breakthrough is always hidden in obedience; your win will not happen without it.

Obedience to GOD makes all the difference.

BUT FIRST, THIS...

How can you obey if you cannot hear instructions? How else could you do as GOD does if you don't know what He's doing? Hearing and knowing what GOD requires of us in every situation is very important to living a winning life. We essentially must learn to become copycats — simply doing and speaking as we hear. When you become GOD's echo, then your life will reflect the kind of win that Jesus saw in His life as a man.

How do you find or recognize GOD's voice when you don't know what He sounds like? By the grace of the Holy Spirit. He is the only one that awakens us to what we don't know but need to know. He alone can make us conscious of His voice. . I thought, 'if I could only hear GOD, then my life would be smooth sailing from then on'; I would know His heart in every situation and that would be my key to winning. I was convinced GOD spoke to everyone — not just a select few — and for the first time I realized it included me, so I sought for it with all my heart and all my strength. And when it finally happened, I heard Him say "It's not about hearing me, it's more about heeding" I was shocked mainly because I could have missed it. It was so different from what I thought it would be. It was not thunderous or earth-shakingly loud like I have seen depicted in movies. It was a distinct, familiar, gentle, and soothing whisper. I knew it was Him, especially because of what He said to me. One way you will know it's GOD is that the wisdom being imparted to you is simply too marvelous for your mind to have thought it up.

It was especially interesting to me the very first time I recognized GOD's voice. His whisper to me was about obedience. I believe it's because obedience is crucial to His agenda for my life. And while I may not know much about your life, I can tell you without a shadow of doubt that obedience is key to yours as well. Through my experience, I've realized simply hearing GOD would not make the difference I sought for my life. Hearing and heeding was the key. Simply knowing GOD's heart concerning a matter does not guarantee we will heed to the same. Nothing changes until we follow through on what we have heard from Him. In that encounter, I also understood His instruction to me on obedience was GOD's mercy poured out in words. He knows too well that to whom much is given, much more is expected, and He expects us to be obedient, having heard. As a matter of fact, it becomes our responsibility to obey immediately we hear Him speak, following His instructions to a T. I also realized many times GOD protects us by keeping His words to Himself because He knows we haven't been trained in obedience yet. He wants us to begin to exercise ourselves in it, so the gift of hearing may not turn into a curse in its misuse.

••••••••

"Why wouldn't it work!", a friend of mine exclaimed one day, as we discussed obedience to GOD. "It must work because we are simply actualizing what GOD wants done." I absolutely agree with him. When we live in obedience and follow through on GOD's instructions, we cannot but win. But first we must hear.

You must desire not to only hear GOD, but to sense Him. Hearing GOD is just one aspect of the senses He has given us to receive and understand His dealings with us. We must desire to hear, see, taste, smell, feel, and perceive Him, in all the ways He has made available for man to sense Him. When we desire a thing, it means we have valued it. So, when it is given to us, we appreciate it because we know its worth. We obviously do not value what we do not desire and so if given to us, we disregard and, sometimes, discard it. But by so doing, what was meant to do us some good becomes useless. Imagine me bringing over your least favorite dish. Would you appreciate it? You wouldn't think much of it, and would probably feed it to your dog once I leave. Now imagine I brought over your favorite dish, and you'd been craving it for days. It is safe to say you will not only appreciate it, but it would blissfully satisfy your hunger.

Hunger always precedes satisfaction. Even the Bible says: *"Blessed are those who hunger and thirst after righteousness, for they will be satisfied"*. I strongly believe we must start with hunger! I usually do this when I'm on to something...I chew on it constantly. Morning, noon, and night, I was knocking on heaven's gates for one thing: the ability to hear GOD for myself. I was madly hungry, I needed to hear Him for myself. I knew an inexhaustible GOD is the only answer to an insatiable hunger. And so, I pressed in, led by the Holy Spirit, just yearning to hear.

All the while I was asking to hear GOD, never did the thought cross my mind until that still-small whisper. His voice was particularly familiar to me, I guess because we never really forget the old voice from the time we dwelt with Him, before the foundations of the world. Also, as I later realized, He had been speaking the whole time. I just wasn't conscious enough to realize it, neither was I yearning after Him at the time, so it was easy to miss. No desire = no expectations. No expectations = missing it when 'it' comes knocking.

From that day, even until now, I pray earnestly for the grace to obey. In the same way, you must pray because obedience is the key to every breakthrough you seek. Pray ceaselessly and you will grow in GOD constantly. But also understand He'll increasingly say even more difficult things to believe or do, and yet we must obey His every word. It doesn't matter how illogical it may sound, just trust Him and follow through. I can guarantee if it's GOD, it will always work out.

NOT WITHOUT WORKS

Obedience is not without work. In fact, it requires hard work. You cannot afford to obey for a season and be careless thereafter. Exercise yourself in obedience, and let it prove GOD perfectly in you. To do so, you must not get weary of obeying. Some get tired of doing good when it takes too long to bear fruit, but we mustn't get weary. We cannot afford to get tired. Breakthrough is just around the corner!

Elijah was a man bristling with confidence in the GOD he served. In his time, he performed many miracles in the name of GOD. But could you imagine what would have happened if Elijah stopped looking out for the rain after his ordeal on the mount in 1 Kings, chapter 18? If he had given up on the sixth try, he would have missed the joy of the seventh. If you give up on the twentieth try, you miss out on the heaven-ordained joy of the twenty-first.

Obedience requires that you do stuff, you know; burn energy! Most times, GOD gives us detailed instructions. So, you must carry out those instructions to partake of the promise in them. For example, when GOD gave Noah instructions to build the ark, his obedience wouldn't have been complete if he didn't build the ark the way God wanted him to build it. Noah put in the required time, resources, and energy in obeying God's instructions. But can you imagine the amount of work required to build that ark? To paint a clearer picture, check out the full-size ark at ARKencounter.com. The first time I saw it, I suddenly felt the weight of the amount of work needed by Noah and his family members to accomplish such a daunting task. Just writing down those measurements would have tired me out, let alone the actual building of the ark. Sometimes, just the mere thought of work requires energy. But Noah didn't tire out on God's instructions. It was a great work. It was focused work. And it sure took sheer determination. But he took it seriously and worked out GOD's instructions.

Many times, people pray but don't go to work on GOD's word. May I ask: having prayed for your heart's desire, what's the next thing you expect to happen? Do you think whatever you have prayed for will automatically drop from the sky? Or will it be delivered to your doorstep? Unfortunately, it doesn't work that way. More than just letters of requests to the Most High GOD, prayers are conversations with GOD through which we align with His will on earth. Prayer calibrates and aligns our mind with the Spirit of GOD. In other words, it ensures we truly have the mind of Christ. In prayer, GOD trades our myopia for His omniscience. So, once we get the revelation in His omniscience, we must set to work; get to building like Noah. But again, obedience is not an easy fix. It is tough work!

I'll end this chapter by sharing a prayer GOD taught me:

'Lord let my ears hear Your counsel and allow my heart (mind) embrace and receive it as Your counsel and Lord, please empower my person (body, mind and spirit) to carry out Your counsel. This I ask, in Jesus' name. Amen'.

8

COME AWAKE

B randon Heath's *Give Me Your Eyes* is a song I really love. It's a request for GOD to give us His eyes so we can see what we've been missing. This implies there are things within reach but out of sight, or, worse still, within sight but out of reach. These days, there are many things going on to which we may be unaware. It's not a problem, if such things have nothing to do with us or will not have a negative impact on us. However, if these things have the ability to make, break, improve, or transform our lives, and how we live it, then it becomes imperative for us to see these things we've been missing.

MORE CONSCIOUS

A friend once asked me to take a quick look around my room. She then proceeded to ask me to tell her how many things were red, with my eyes closed. As I started to think about the red items in the room, I initially drew a blank. I eventually remembered one thing, so I answered "one". But once I could open my eyes to count, I was amazed at how many red things were in the room! I counted 5! Suddenly I remembered every single one of them; I even remembered how they each became part of my room. In that moment, I came to a new understanding: though we may see, we are not conscious of everything within our line of sight. Those additional red things I counted did not suddenly appear in my room just when I was asked to count with my eyes opened. They had always been there. When I looked around the first time, I'm sure my eyes grazed over them, but their existence did not register in my brain at all. I saw them but I didn't 'see' them. Now if that's the case with physical sight, which we think we have mastered over the years, I can't help but wonder just how much more we're unconscious of in the spirit. How much have we missed out on because we just didn't 'see'?

In explaining the parable of the sower to His disciples, Jesus said to them "*To you, it has been given to know the mystery of the kingdom of God; but to those who are outside, all things come in parables, so that [in] seeing, they may see and not perceive, and [in] hearing, they may hear and not understand….*" I believe this implies it's possible to see (as I could see my room) and yet not perceive. It implies you can hear all that's said around you and simply be in the dark about the truth being shared. In this context, the words 'perceive' and 'understand' speak to the process of taking in the information so that you can put it to use in your life. We cannot act on what we do not understand, nor can our decisions be influenced by what is not perceived. If I were going to be awarded a prize for being able to tell how many red things were in my room that day, I would have gone home empty handed.

In life, there is a prize we will miss out on if we are not conscious, perceptive, and understand all that is present around us. We will miss out on the fulfilled and successful life we ought to live out in the world. Everything that exists plays a part in helping us express the fullness within. When we begin to sense all that exists, decode them and make healthy decisions based on them all, we begin to live in the fullness of our winning life. We can no longer afford to see without perceiving or hear without understanding. It's chipping away at our win. We must begin to see and perceive so that we can put to good use what we have seen.

The difference between seeing and perceiving can be explained in the difference between knowledge and understanding. Unless we understand a truth, and believe in its content, simply knowing it doesn't do us any good. For example, many people are familiar with this seemingly simple equation on the correlation between mass and energy, $E = mc^2$. But I wonder how many people truly understand what it means. And only those who 'see' and 'understand' the equation can translate it into something meaningful. One of the most relatable (in my opinion) applications of this simple equation is by Joshua Carrol. On his blog, Universe Today, a site dedicated to space and astronomy, he used this equation to give his readers good insight on the potential energy in a human being based on their body weight in kilograms. By the time he was done his calculations, he stated that a man who weighs about

190 lbs. has about 7.8 septillion joules of energy in his body; that's approximately 7,8000,000,000,000,000,000,000 in numeric format. Now, that's a lot of energy! And to put it in perspective, he concluded that a single man has about 1.86 Million times the energy in the explosive material, TNT.

He was only able to apply this concept so well, even to basic and relatable things, because he understood the concept behind the equation. We also need to understand the concept behind many of life's equations so that we can apply them properly to different areas of our lives. We must sense, and then use what is sensed to help us make better decisions and judgments in all situations. If we come to knowledge without understanding, we are just like a person who doesn't even know at all. If all we do is see, and we do not perceive, we are not better off than the one who can't see. And if we hear without understanding, we are just like the deaf.

But if we pay attention, we can find hope in that same scripture!

Jesus says to us (remember to personalize the scriptures): "To you, it has been given to know the mystery of the kingdom of God". To us it has been given to 'know mysteries' — to see and perceive, to hear and understand, to sense and decode the mysteries of the kingdom. We have been given the grace to go further than just seeing. This is the gift from The Most High; that we will not only search and find, but see and perceive, hear and understand! Remember, not all who see, perceive, not all who hear, understand,

and not all who seek will find. But because of the gift and the promise, and especially because He gifted Himself to us, we can be sure of the perception and understanding in all things. This is because we no longer see through our own eyes, nor do we perceive based on our own understanding. But everything is now seen, perceived, and understood through GOD's eyes, through His ears, and by the understanding of the Holy Spirit who is alive within us.

SLEEPWALKERS

I noticed a while ago that I didn't have a good recollection of my childhood. I mean, I remember the big events; things that were significant, and the things that were particularly strange; — just no details. And for someone who is tuned to details, it seems especially strange my memory of things as it pertains to my childhood is so vague and scattered. I mean, most of my childhood is a complete wash in my head. When my siblings talk about some events from our childhood, they recall things as though it happened yesterday. Me? Not even the faintest clue. Sometimes, they can't believe I can't remember. To them, these events were significant enough to stick to their memories; my response to them is a look as though to say. "sorry, I can't help you". It didn't bother me much at first. I didn't even think anything of it. That is until I realized it was a result of living life unconsciously for so long — I had been sleep-walking through life and I didn't even know it!

•••••••

In somnology — the study of sleep — there are 3 stages of sleep. Stage 1 is called the Alpha stage. This is the stage of sleep when one is just starting to drift off but still a bit conscious of the environment. In this stage, the sleeper is between two states: sleep and awake. The body is relaxed and getting ready to sleep.

Stage 2 is when one falls asleep. The person is no longer aware of their surroundings and they are simply sleeping. In this stage of sleep, you can be awoken with ease. I would guess those who are light sleepers spend most of their sleep time in this stage. So, while they are truly sleeping they can be easily woken by the smallest of sounds.

Stage 3 is when you are in deep sleep. In this stage, it becomes difficult to be awoken. I am told everyone goes through these phases, all night long — kind of like stepping up a ladder and then coming down immediately, repeating the pattern over and over again. I was also told by my sister, who happened to have read up on the topic, that sleepwalking occurs in stage 3.

Sleepwalking happens when someone who is sound asleep suddenly, without consciousness of their real environment, begins to act out what's going on in their dreams. While they may be moving, walking and talking, they are not aware they are still asleep. When this happens, you can imagine their actions will not match the situation at hand in their physical reality. I once heard of a woman who, during one of her sleepwalking episodes, sprayed her bed with the fire extinguisher. When she came to, she said, in her dream, her bed was on fire and she was trying to put it out. Regardless of how real her dreams seemed to her on that day, the fact remains she was not awake, and only those who are truly awake can tell the difference. The same thing goes for those who are sleepwalking through life. They do not realize it's all been a sleepwalking episode. They think it's the real deal. And in many cases, the people around them are also sleepwalking, so there is no one to waken them from their sleep-induced actions.

The stages of sleep can help shed some light on the levels of being awake. Based on these stages, you can gather one could be fully awake (when one is not sleeping), partially awake (when one is asleep but awake — like the light sleepers), fully asleep (like the deep sleeper) or fully asleep and acting awake (like the sleepwalkers). The last instance is the absolute worst — and that was me! I was fully asleep but I thought I was fully awake. I acted awake, looked awake, and felt awake. But when I look back, it is crystal clear life was just happening to me. I wasn't playing my part in deciding what happened or didn't happen to me (at least in the capacity in which GOD had given me to do so). Things just happened and I accepted them as such. It was clear I didn't remember most things because I didn't have a part to play in creating them. I didn't decide on them and I didn't partake in them. I was alive and breathing but I wasn't living out life; life was simply passing me by. It is impossible to wake one's self when you do not even realize you're not awake. I couldn't have woken up on my own; The One who never sleeps nor slumbers — The One who is truly awake — woke me up to life. And when He did, it was clear that I hadn't been awake all the while.

Many people are currently where I was. They think they are awake because they can see. They think they are awake because they can hear. They think they are awake because they are not physically sleeping. But just like I was, many are sleepwalking - awake in the natural but spiritually asleep. Awake as they know it, but absent from the life they ought to be living in Christ.

You can't afford to sleepwalk through life

WAKE UP

> *"Now the angel who talked with me came back and wakened me, as a man who is wakened out of his sleep. And he said to me, "What do you see?" So, I said, "I am looking, and there is a lampstand of solid gold with a bowl on top of it, and on the stand seven lamps with seven pipes to the seven lamps. Two olive trees are by it, one at the right of the bowl and the other at its left." So, I answered and spoke to the angel who talked with me, saying, "What are these, my lord?" Then the angel who talked with me answered and said to me, "Do you not know what these are?" And I said,*
> *"No, my lord." (Zechariah 4:1-5 NKJV)*

The Angel in the passage above had been speaking to Zechariah for a long time. In Chapter 1, the "Angel of the Lord" told Zechariah GOD had made up His mind to restore the peace and beauty of

Jerusalem and put a stop to their affliction. In Chapter 2, this same angel spoke to him about the expansion of Jerusalem, even into a city without walls, a city in which GOD would be its walls, and a wall of fire at that. In Chapter 3, Zechariah saw a vision of and heard the Angel speak of the promises to remove the inquiry of Jerusalem and establish His promises concerning her. So, it seems a bit strange that, suddenly, the same Angel returns to Zechariah, and taps him with the intent to awaken him, as though he was sleeping. It seems strange, but could it be he was jolting Zechariah up into a whole new level of awakening? Could it be Zechariah was not fully awake and he needed a greater awakening state than he currently was in?

I believe Zechariah was in one level of consciousness, and the angel needed him to come awake into a higher level of consciousness. I believe until that point, Zechariah was seeing, but not quite perceiving, he was beholding awesome sights in the visions before him, but perhaps he was not taking in the fullness of what was being exposed to him. Zechariah thought he was awake, but he needed to be awakened; that's why the Angel jolted him awake. The point here is this: just because we are beholding amazing sights doesn't mean we are awake; even sleepwalkers are seeing great things but they're unconscious of what they see.

The angel prompted Zechariah, just as my friend prompted me to what was within sight but not perceived. Her seemingly insignificant exercise guided me to a far greater truth that had eluded me up till that time. My hope is this exercise does the same for you too. It's important you also come awake. Come awake from sleep mode so you can begin to live the fullness of the life you were designed for. We need to be awake and conscious of all that's around us, the worlds within our reach, and the realms we exist in. We need to take in all of that and make decisions that will bring about the fullness of GOD in our lives.

WHO WILL TEACH IT?

How do you recognize what you are looking for when you don't know what it looks like? This question dropped into my heart a few years ago and I haven't recovered from it yet. I hope I never do. This was one of those moments when you realize GOD's reality shatters everything you think you know. But honestly, how do you recognize what you have never seen? The very essence of the word 'recognize' is to remember something based on past experiences or foreknowledge. To recognize implies we have seen it before and can rely on our memory of it. In this case, we can't rely on the past, neither is there anything to recollect. All our experiences will not help us figure out what we have never seen before. So how then do we recognize it? Now, that's a GOD question!

When GOD asks mind-blowing questions like these, I have learnt to answer like Ezekiel. "Only you know, Lord." That was his answer when the Lord took him to a valley filled with very dry human skeletons. In the face of such dryness and lifelessness, GOD asked, "Ezekiel, can these bones live?" Ezekiel answered with such great wisdom, "...only you know, Lord". What else could he say? GOD was asking Ezekiel about life, when all he could see was death. But God was specifically asking him: can you look past the signal your eyes are sending to your brain concerning what is in front of you? Can you defy logic and everything you know? Can you get past the knowledge in your head and look to me for possibilities?

If I could paraphrase GOD's response to Ezekiel it would be this: "By Me, they will". And by Him we will too! We will only recognize what we are looking for with GOD. And when we do, it will seem familiar! They'll be familiar because they've always been there (just like the red items in my room were suddenly familiar when my eyes were opened). You've always seen it but didn't recognize it. You've always heard it but didn't understand it. You've always known it, you just didn't perceive it. You have never seen, heard nor known them in the light in which you will now. GOD is that light through which you see old things in new ways. You will only recognize it by The Holy Spirit.

Let GOD alone lead you. Only He truly knows the way.

The Bible talks about a narrow path that leads to life. It says, "...only a few find it." Have you ever wondered why only a few find it? I believe it's because this path requires us to let GOD take the lead. He created this path, He hid it, He can find it and He will lead you there. Trust me when I say, what you are looking for is right there in plain sight; it's always within sight. But it might have been out of reach until now. The few who find it are those awakened and led by the Spirit of GOD! Now, let Him lead you there!

9

WHAT MORE!

As simple as writing a book may sound, there's more to it than just having a focal idea or coming up with an outline for the idea. Having given a series of teachings on these simple but mighty principles, you would think documenting these teachings would be a piece of cake, right? No, far from it. On most days, the process felt like I was travailing with child. It wasn't too difficult to write. Actually, writing was the simplest part (simple is definitely not easy in this case). What I found to be the hardest part of writing was being able to translate 'spirit' into English. Finding the right words to convey what was in my heart was the hardest on most days. If you have ever tried translating words or ideas from one language to another, you would understand what I mean. Often, you'll find that in translations, you run the risk of losing important details with certain words and ideas, and therefore one requires a certain level of meticulousness.

When GOD speaks, usually it's in the simplest of words, but

they come with great understanding; and translating these 'understandings' sometimes can be a task. It was difficult being subjected to the mental travailing I experienced to birth this baby you now hold in your hands. Many of those days it took GOD's encouragement and mental buffing to get past the mental trolls that would ask me who I thought I was to be writing a book. Those thoughts came in harsher words but I resolved to stand against them every step of the way. If I can be honest with you, the time of writing this crowning chapter was the most difficult of all. But that's not surprising, because the last few minutes of pushing a baby through the birth canal can be the most difficult.

•••••••

On my first birthing trip to the hospital, I had gone into labor two nights before my expected delivery date. I was excited, eager to meet our little bundle of joy. I didn't think much about the process since I had never experienced it before. I mean, how bad could it be, right? I knew it wouldn't be a day in the park but boy, nothing could have prepared me for what I actually experienced. Due to all my research on epidurals, I had made up my mind that the risk associated with taking a large needle in my spine was too great for me. So, I was going to do deliver my baby drug-free. When the real pain kicked in, all I could think about was the pain. I probably could have changed my mind, to take the epidural, but the pain from the contractions was so mind-numbing that I didn't even remember I had that option. And before you think the pain was the height of it, the crescendo came hours later when I had to push *through* the pain. Almost eight hours into the whole thing, I was weak, drained and I really didn't want to have a baby anymore at that point. I said to my doctor "I can't push anymore, I am exhausted" and I'll never forget her response to me: "you can't say that," she said, almost scared that I could even think to give up. "Push, harder" she concluded. And somehow, with my husband and sister by my side, praying fervently, and with GOD Himself empowering me through the process, I got another wind of strength, gave one last powerful push, and pleaded with my son to come forth. I was literally calling him forth, and voila! He broke through every barrier, and his whole body came flying out in an instant. I didn't realize I had anything left in me, but when the doctor said 'push', my spirit heard 'fight!'.

What more? Fight! Fight to win! Push through on these principles. That's all that's left to do. Life is a battle at which you must win; there can be no other outcome. When you engage life with the right tools, and live by the right principles, according to The Creator's design, you are sure to win. If you are reading this book, you've been chosen to participate in the battle of life and you really don't have a choice now; you are here already. You may have had a choice before you came into this world, but at this point, 'tag! you are it'. You are already in it. Now fight!

You must fight to win. You can't win if you don't fight. The very definition of a win implies the existence of a fight, or some sort of a battle in which a victor has now come forth. While I'm sure I've ingrained it into your thoughts by now that life is simple with GOD, and as I always append "simple, not easy", here is the "not easy" part: the fight. It's not enough to be a player on the sidelines, you will not be eligible for the win if you seat on the sidelines or give up your spot in this fight. Fight hard. Don't give up, don't give in; fight! You are sure to win!

If you must fight, fight to win

SHADOWBOXING

This fight is not a cat fight where you aim at all directions and anything goes; you need to be particularly strategic about your fight. You can't fight every battle either; you only need to fight the ones GOD has chosen for you. And you can bet if GOD chooses that battle for you, you are sure to win. He would never lead you into a defeat. Don't spread yourself thin and lose every battle because you have not channeled your efforts with precision. Deliver your effort into the right things to ensure your win in this battle called life. If you search the records from Genesis to Revelation, you'll find that every GOD-led battle resulted in a win. The only battles the children of Israel ever lost were battles GOD didn't want them engaged in, or battles in which they didn't follow the strategic plan and instructions GOD laid out for them. You can be sure of your win in life when GOD is leading you. But you must stick to His laid-out plan for that win. It's important to not fight like one that's shadowboxing, swinging at everything and rumbling down every path without aim.

This fight you're in is more like boxing than anything else. It's funny that I should use boxing analogies here, because as a young girl, I didn't like boxing at all. I used to cry watching people beating themselves black and blue. But as I grew older, I came to respect the sport, although I wouldn't consider myself a boxing fan just yet. But one of the reasons boxing later gained my respect was the fact that the boxer's win is heavily dependent on his strategies. Every great boxer spends time not only in preparation through training and sharpening their boxing techniques, but also in their win strategy. From the little I know of boxing, preparation always precedes victory, but the boxing strategy is the victory sealant. Strategy is how control is established in the ring; by them are wins secured. One common strategy that's used in boxing is throwing strong blows strategically to known weak spots on the opponent's body to control the game. Like in boxing, you must be intentional and strategic in this fight of your life; your punches must be strong and targeted. You can't afford to just throw strong punches; every punch must be effective for the intended target. That's why Paul says in 1 Corinthians 9:26 and I paraphrase, *I am not fighting with uncertainty for my victory, because I fight with precision; and I do not throw punches all over the place like someone who is boxing the air.* If you must fight, then fight to win. With GOD, there can be no other outcome.

WORD FIGHT

I know what you are thinking. Word fight? We've been taught not to do such. That's one of the lessons my grandma used to ring in my ears when I was little. "Don't engage in a word battle with anyone, it's not a good use of your time" she would say. And thankfully that was never a big challenge for me since I wasn't much of a talker anyway. I know that's a real challenge for some folks, one they ought to learn to put to proper use lest they misuse it. But I am not talking about that type of word fight. Just like everything in life with a negative and positive side, there is a battle of words that is futile and will prove a total misuse of your time but there is one which is most rewarding and can aid your fight to the win.

Think right. Everything we are starts from thought, and being can only begin from feeling. Your feelings are like thoughts of the soul, you've got to think and feel positive. It is critical to your win to pay attention to the thoughts that govern your mind and ensure they align with the win that you are going for. Every thought counts. Don't waste the creative space of your mind dwelling on ideas and thoughts will not aid your win. Refuse every thought contrary to where you are headed and continually renew your mind by speaking the truth of GOD to yourself constantly. Rome wasn't built in a day and neither are the sets of thoughts you have housed in your mind. But you must be diligent at it and clean out the negative thoughts one word at a time. *Watch* every thought or feeling that comes to you, make sure you only entertain those that agree with the reality you must create. *Control* those thoughts or feelings that slip through but do not further your cause. And *alter* every thought that seems to be out of control that seeks to change your destination even your win. Do these consciously and deliberately each day.

Speak right. When you begin to think of every word you utter as a prayer, you'll be cautious of what you say. When you understand prayer is simply a conversation with GOD and you come to the perfect understanding that GOD is omnipresent, meaning He is everywhere, you will know every word you speak whether intended for His hearing or not, are all heard by Him. When you get this understanding you'll know you're in constant communion with GOD. Speak only that which you want to be a prayer into your life, speak only that which you wouldn't mind heaven saying amen to. And be careful what you speak concerning others too because much more than goes out to them comes to you, for every seed is multiplied to the tree that produced it. Remember your tongue is laced with power. The creative breath of The Almighty is upon your lips. Speak it and the world will follow suit. You will be known only as you know yourself. Mohammed Ali dubbed himself 'the greatest', and everyone followed suit. Go ahead dub yourself and the entire universe will follow suit respectfully.

WEAPON OF CHOICE

Your now — this moment — is a fork in the road to where you

are going. At every fork in the road, decisions are made, and the decisions you make are just as important as the ones you don't make. They all go into a big web, spinning your life into being. So choose consciously and choose wisely. Choice is how we change our course when needed. It's not enough to know that you can win, or say that you are a winner, you must choose your win. Make choices that align with what you profess. Don't say one thing and do another thing; that's called fooling yourself.

I once had a dream where I was seated in a classroom with a few other people. The lecturer who represented GOD in my dream, walked in and as she sat down, she began to say, in front of the whole class, all my shortcomings. She was telling all the intimate things I had shared only with GOD and was just blurting it all out in the open. She didn't call my name but I knew she was talking about me. I broke down crying and I remember telling the person seating next to me, "she's talking about me! I haven't hidden any of these things from the Lord, He knows I struggle with all these things". In the dream, I was perplexed. I couldn't understand why GOD would out me like that. After all, I have always been open with whatever I struggled with or still struggle with. When I woke up, I cried some more. The thought of GOD being upset with me was unbearable. I pleaded for mercy, I was distraught and just didn't know what to do. Soon I felt the Lord console me and I was overcome with peace knowing GOD's voice. Whether in praise or in chastening, His voice is His mercy unfolding towards me. I realized I would take His voice, even if it was chastening, over silence; anything but being without Him. I was released from that burden but I couldn't get over the dream's details. I was sure GOD still loved me but I just couldn't understand the public exposure. There was a message hidden in it but I just couldn't decode it.

Months later during a conversation with a friend, it suddenly hit me. GOD exposed me in public in that dream because He was tired of hearing about my struggles; being open about them but doing nothing to change them. That's when He started teaching me about choice. Choice is a weapon through which we fight to the win. Every stronghold of habit, culture, attitude, can be pulled down with the weapon of 'choice'. You must begin to make choices that align with what you believe and profess. You can no longer hide under the cloak of being open with GOD about our struggles. We must go one step further and do something about it with strong and effective tools He has provided us with. The battle between your current state and your desired state cannot be won without this powerful artillery called choice. Your choices are GOD's chosen weapons through which you will transition into your win. The win you desire in your life is a choice away. Be strategic about what you choose.

FIGHT LIKE A MULE

One of my favorite original quotes is "Be mule-like stubborn about your happy". I love it especially because it highlights that stubbornness is not always be a bad thing. There are certain situations where you ought to be unshakably stubborn and your win is definitely one of those situations. There can be no other outcome. This is signed, sealed and delivered by the precious blood of Christ and we must not give it away or lay it down carelessly. There is a time to be compliant and there is a time to be stubborn. Andy Stanley puts it this way: "Stubbornness is a virtue when you are right". When you are right, you ought to be stubborn to follow through on that which you know. Don't let any old thing knock you off your win. Take your win like a mule, don't settle for anything less. No more playing fair with the enemy.

Be mule-like stubborn
about your happy

Some people are playing fair with the devil when he has never been fair a day in his existence. It's time to take it by force! What GOD's got for you is for you. Go and get it! Stump out the mouths of lions if you must, rip them in shreds with your bare hands if that's what's needed. Whatever you do, don't give up! Fight with the assurance that the power alive and working in you is far greater than the power that works in them.

Fight knowing there can be no other outcome. Fight to win!

EPILOGUE

Revelation is truly exciting, and rightfully so. There is something about being privy to hidden or secret information that makes one feel special. For me, revelation is the fulfillment of GOD's promise as stated in Jeremiah 33:3 which reads: *"Call to me and I will answer you and show you great and mighty things, which you do not know."* Revelation is when GOD decides to show us great and mighty things we could never discover on our own. Sometimes, it's an old truth lit up in a new way that revolutionizes how we live. Other times, it's a new discovery, a new truth that uproots the false ideas we had been grounded in. Either way, revelation is a gift from the Lord, and, indeed, blessed are its readers, hearers, and keepers!

I know you must have had many eureka moments in your journey through the pages of this book. I hope that you encountered revelation after revelation, and are as wide-eye-opened in awe as I was when they were first spoken to me. And I know that even greater revelations will be revealed to you as you take to God's word in these pages. One of the things I love about the Holy Spirit is His ability to exponentially multiply our understanding, even as we encounter His words. He literally shapes a new world out of them; a better world than the writer or speaker can convey. Because of what The Holy Spirit does with words, I've been blessed in more ways than intended by the authors of some books I've read. My sincere heart's desire for every reader that picks up this book is that it catapults you into much deeper, broader, and higher revelations than I can imagine penning down. I pray The Holy Spirit will multiply every word and bring you into a reality beyond the excitement the words have created within you. So, I want to urge you to go one up from revelation. Because as great and exciting as that is, it's only an invitation.

The sole purpose of revelation is to alter experience. When GOD unveils truths to us, our part is to receive and put them to use in our lives so they can alter the experiences we would have had otherwise. For example, when GOD reveals the good ahead to us, it becomes our responsibility to follow instructions so that we can partake of that very good. And when He reveals the evil ahead to us, it's our responsibility to duck and avert that experience. Proverbs 10:8 says, "The wise in heart will accept and obey counsel but the foolish of lips will fall headlong." Use the counsel given to you in this book for the purpose of a fuller, richer, grander win. All the exponential knowledge that The Holy Spirit multiples, the renewing of your mind that happens through revelation, as well as the excitement that crowns the process, are all to one end: a better, greater life experience. We must begin to experience better, greater and fuller lives than what we're used to experiencing. And you are at the right place to be able to do that.

I am sure you are excited about all you have read, but please get even more excited. Enough to work. Enough to run after every word. Enough to grab hold of the possibility of your win. And enough to not only know that a great win is possible but to experience that kind of win in your life. Don't get too excited about the invitation and forget the experience it calls you into. Honor this invitation and be present at your feast!

QUOTABLES

Share your favorite quotes using these hashtags
#SecretsToWin #MyWinNow
Below are a few more of mine:

GOD's joy can only
be full, in its entirety
over your life when
you win here on earth
as well as in heaven.

•••••••

Your most profound
'why' is to manifest GOD

•••••••

When we misuse a thing,
we are bound to think
it's difficult or hard or
simply not meant for us.

Regardless of how you
feel about it, life hasn't
been rigged against
you; it isn't a tcasc; and
it isn't a punishment...
it's an assignment.

·······

Life will continue
to seem complicated
until you get it.

·······

Life was designed for
you, not against you.

·······

Just when you think
you've gotten to
the end of the rope,
GOD extends it.

GOD is bent on your
win more than He is
bent on keeping you
at bay for your sins
and shortcomings.

•••••••

Humility is always the
cure for humiliation.

•••••••

Kids are channels
through which GOD
teaches their parents.

•••••••

Faith is not the absence
of doubt; it is simply
the conscious choice
of an assured hope.

To nourish a tree you
must go to the roots;
the same is true when
you want to uproot it.

. . . .

A simple reorganization
of your viewpoint about
any situation can make a
mountain of difference.

. . . .

When you become
GOD's echo, you will
see the same results
in your life that Jesus
experienced in His

. . . .

The best things in life are
not just free; GOD has
also made them simple.

NOTES

Chapter 1

Pg 1: Leaping from glory to glory (2 Corinthians 3:18 KJV)
Pg 13: *"What is man that You are mindful of him…"* (Psalm 8:4-9 NKJV)
Pg 14: *"As the rain and the snow come down fro…"* (Isaiah 55:10-11 NIV)
Pg 14: When GOD said *"Light"* in the beginning (Genesis 1:3 MSG)
Pg 15: *"No word from GOD shall be without power…"* (Luke 1:37 AMPC)

Chapter 2

Pg 19: "If you can do anything…" (Mark 9:24 NIV)
Pg 20: Elijah & the prophets of Baal (1 Kings 18: 20-29)
Pg 22: "You must never doubt..." V. Raymond Edman
Pg 23: *"Blessed are they who have believed…"* (John 20:29 NIV)
Pg 24: *"If you, then, though you are evil…"* (Matthew 7:11 NIV)
Pg 25: When Jesus came down from… (Matthew 8:1-3 NIV)
Pg 29: *"Blessed is she who believed, for there …"* (Luke 1:45 NKJV)
Pg 30: *"My sheep hear my voice…"* (John 10:4-5)
Pg 31: The Way, The Truth and The Life (John 1:46)
Pg 31: I believe! Please help my unbelief (Mark 9:24 KJV)

Chapter 3

Pg 34: Our latter would be greater than the former (Haggai 2:9)
Pg 34: *"So you, my son, be strong…"* (2 Timothy 2:1-7 AMP)
Pg 37: *"Faith is the assurance of things hoped for...."* (Hebrews 11:1 AMP)
Pg 38: Faith comes by hearing (Romans 10:17)
Pg 38: *"And the earth was without form, and void…"* (Genesis 1:2 KJV)
Pg 39: "In Him all things consist" (Colossians 1:17)
Pg 40: Shall two work together unless they agree? (Amos 3:3)
Pg 44: "Be it far from you Lord" (Matthew 16:22 NKJV)
Pg 51: If your eyes cause you to err, pluck it out (Matthew 18:9)
Pg 51: "If any of you lack wisdom, let him ask…" (James 1:5 NKJV)

Chapter 4

Pg 56: Jesus was walking by a fig tree. (Mark 11:12-25)
Pg 57: Out of wine at the wedding in Canaan (John 2:1-12)
Pg 57: *"My time has not come yet"* (John 2:4 NLT)
Pg 59 His thoughts towards you..." (Jeremiah 29:11)
Pg 59: *"I tell you the truth, if you have faith...* (Matthew 21:21 NLT)
Pg 63: *"The people that know their GOD..."* (Daniel 11:32 NKJV)
Pg 63: "...not fold arms" – Seun Akinlotan of Onpoint Success
Pg 64: *"David left his things with…."* (1 Samuel 17:20-51 NLT)
Pg 66: With GOD all things are possible. (Matthew 19:26)
Pg 67: He is very familiar with our infirmities.... (Hebrews 4:15)
Pg 68: Out of your belly will flow rivers of living waters. (John 7:38)
Pg 69: Don't lean on our own understanding (Proverbs 3:5)
Pg 69: *Then the LORD God formed..." (Genesis 2:7-9, 15-17 NLT).*
Pg 73: GOD has not given us... (2 Timothy 1:7)
Pg 75: *"You are the salt of the earth..."* (Matthew 5:13 NKJV)
Pg 75: *"Our lives are…."* (2 Corinthians 2:15 NLT)
Pg 76: *"To those who …"* (2 Corinthians 2:16 NLT)
Pg 77: "Our deepest fear..." Marianne Williamson
Pg 78: *"In all thy getting,..."* (Proverbs 4:7 KJV)

Chapter 5

Pg 80: *"There is no such thing as impossible, the word itself says I'm possible"* – Audrey Hepburn
Pg 84: *"My grace is sufficient…."* (2 Corinthians 12:9 AMP)
Pg 85: *"I am glad to boast about…".* (2 Corinthians 12:9 AMP)
Pg 88: A wise man sees a ditch ahead…. (Proverbs 27:12)
Pg 88: Jacob & Esau and the birth right (Genesis 27)
Pg 89: *"But when you decide to break...""* (Genesis 27:40 NLT)
Pg 95: GOD is the sun of our lives… (John1:1-5).

Chapter 6

Pg 97: "My people are destroyed... (Hosea 4:6 KJV)
Pg 98: "You must not eat from..." (Genesis 2:17 NIV)
Pg 99: "You have heard that..." (Matthew 5:27 NKJV)
Pg 103: "Whosoever is born of GOD..." (1 John 3:9 NKJV)
Pg 105: "Who is my mother...?" (Matthew 12:46-50 NKJV)
Pg 106: "[a] good tree bears good..." (Matthew 7:18 NIV)

Chapter 7

Pg 110: As far as the heavens are... (Psalm 103:11)
Pg 114: "If Jesus did all He sis as man - Bill Johnson
        (from a sermon I heard sometime ago)
Pg 115: ".... once has GOD spoken..." (Psalm 62:11 NLT)
Pg 115: "I tell you the truth, the Son…" (John 5:19 NLT)
Pg 115: "He humbled himself …." (Philippians 2:8-11 AMP)
Pg 119: "Blessed are those who…." (Matthew 5:7 NKJV).
Pg 121: GOD gave Noah instructions to build the ark
        (Genesis 6:14)

Chapter 8

Pg 123: Give me yours (song) What if we (Album)
        Brandon Heath (Singer/Songwriter)
Pg 124: *"To you, it has been…."* (Matthew 13:11 KJV)
Pg 125: Universetoday.com – Joshua Caroll's blog
Pg 130: "Now the angel who…." (Zechariah 4:1-5 NKJV)
Pg 132: "Only you know, Lord." (Ezekiel 37:3 NKJV)
Pg 133: "...only a few find it." (Matthew 7:14 NIV)

Notes...

Chapter 9

Pg 139: *I am not fighting...* (1 Corinthians 9:26)
Pg 144: "stubbornness is a virtue..." — Andy Stanley

Epilogue

Pg 145: "Call to me and I will ..." (Jeremiah 33:3 NKJV)
Pg 146: "The wise in heart will ..." (Proverbs 10:8)

AUTHOR

Find TemitOpe online at www.temitopeibrahim.com.
On Facebook at www.facebook.com/temitopeibrahim75
On Instagram @iamfaraboverubies